THE
VOLUNTARYIST CREED

BEING THE HERBERT SPENCER LECTURE

DELIVERED AT OXFORD, JUNE 7, 1906

AND

A PLEA FOR VOLUNTARYISM

BY

AUBERON HERBERT

PRINTED FOR W. J. SIMPSON

AT THE OXFORD UNIVERSITY PRESS

LONDON. HENRY FROWDE

AMEN CORNER E.C.

1908

Originally published in 1908.

Large Print Edition published 2012 by Skyler J. Collins.
Visit: www.skylerjcollins.com

Cover image by StockFreeImages.com.

ISBN-13: 978-1479305780
ISBN-10: 1479305782

The first of the two papers which this book contains is the Herbert Spencer Lecture delivered by Mr. Auberon Herbert in the Sheldonian Theatre at Oxford on June 7, 1906.

The second paper was only completed by Mr. Herbert a few days before his death in November, 1906. He had intended to circulate this summary of the Voluntaryist Creed for signature by those who agreed with it.

MR. SPENCER AND THE
GREAT MACHINE

I

I BEGAN my lecture at Oxford by expressing my sense of the debt that we owed to Mr. Spencer for his splendid attempt to show us the great meanings that underlie all things—the order, the intelligibility, the coherence, that exist in this world of ours. I confessed that, on some great points of his philosophy, I differed from his teaching, parting, so to speak, at right angles from him; but that difference did not alter my view of how much he had helped us in the clear bold way in which he had traced the great principles running through the like and unlike things of our world; and in which with so skilful a hand he had grouped the facts round those principles, that he always followed—might I say—with the keen instinct of a hound that follows the scent of the prey in front of him. Time, I thought, might take away much, and might add much; but the effort to unite all parts of the great whole, to bind and connect them all together, would remain as a splendid monument of what one man, treading a path of his own, could achieve.

But to-day we are only concerned with his social and political teaching, where we may, I think, follow his leading with more reliance, and with but little reserve. I have often laughed and said that, as far as I myself was concerned, he spoilt my political life. I went into the House of Commons, as a young man, believing that we might do much for the people by a bolder and more unsparing use of the powers that belonged to the great law-making machine ; and great, as it then seemed to me, were those still unexhausted resources of united national action on behalf of the common welfare. It was at that moment that I had the privilege of meeting Mr. Spencer, and the talk which we had—a talk that will always remain very memorable to me—set me busily to work to study his writings. As I read and thought over what he taught, a new window was opened in my mind. I lost my faith in the great machine ; I saw that thinking and acting for others had always hindered not helped the real progress ; that all forms of compulsion deadened the living forces in a nation ; that every evil violently stamped out still persisted, almost always in a worse form, when driven out of sight, and festered under the surface. I no longer believed that the handful of us—however well-intentioned we might be—spending our nights in the House, could manufacture the life of a nation, could endow it out of hand with happiness, wisdom and prosperity, and clothe it in all the virtues. I began to see that we were only playing with an imaginary magician's wand ; that the ambitious work we were trying to do lay far out of the reach of our hands, far, far, above the small measure of our strength. It was a work that could only be done in one way—not by gifts and doles of public money, not by making that most corrupting and demoralizing of all things, a common purse ; not by restraints and compulsions of each other ; not by seeking to move in a mass, obedient to the strongest forces of the moment, but by acting through the living energies of the free individuals left free to combine in their own way, in their own groups, finding their own experience, setting before themselves their own hopes and desires, aiming only at such ends as they truly shared in common, and ever as the foundation of it all, respecting deeply and religiously alike their own freedom, and the freedom of all others. And if it was not in our power,—we excellent and worthy people,—fighting our nightly battle of words, with our half-light, our patchwork of knowledge, and our party passions, often swayed, in a great measure unconsciously, by our own interests, half autocrats, half puppets, if it was not given to us to create progress, in any true sense of the word, and to present it to the nation, ready-made, fresh from our ever busy anvil, much in the fashion that kind-hearted nurses hand out cake and jam to expectant children ; if all this taking of a nation's life out of its own hands into our hands was but a bewildered dream, a careless conceit on our part, might it not, on the other hand, be only too easily in our power to mislead and to injure, to hinder and destroy the voluntary self-helping efforts and experiments that were beyond all price, to depress the great qualities, to soften and break down the national fibre, and in the end, as we flung our gifts broadcast, to turn the whole people into two or three reckless quarrelling crowds, that had lost all confidence in their own qualities and resources, that were content to remain dependent on what others did for them—ever disappointed, ever discontented, because the natural and healthy field of their own energies had been closed to them, and all that they now had to do was to clamour as loudly as possible for each new thing that their favourite speakers hung in glittering phrases before their eyes ? I saw that no guiding, no limiting or moderating principle existed in the competition of politician against politician ; but that almost all hearts were filled with the old corrupting desire, that had so long haunted the world for its ceaseless sorrow, to possess that evil mocking gift of power, and to use it in their own imagined interest—without question, without scruple—over their fellow men. From that day I gave myself to preaching, in my own small way, the saving doctrine of liberty, of self-ownership and self-guidance, and of resisting that lust for power, which had brought such countless sufferings and misfortunes on all races in the past, and which still, to-day, turns the men and women of the same country, who should be as friends and close allies, if the word 'country' has any meaning, into two hostile armies, ever wastefully, uselessly, and to the destruction of their own happiness and prosperity, striving against each other, always dreading, often hating, those whom the fortunes of war may at any moment make their masters. Was it for this—this bitter, reckless and rather sordid warfare—I tried to ask—that we were leading this wonderful earth-life; was this the true end, the true fulfilment of all the great qualities and nobler ambitions that belonged to our nature?

Now, whether you judge that I acted rightly or wrongly in thus yielding myself to Mr. Spencer's influence, you will not, I think, quarrel very seriously with me, if I say that between Mr. Spencer's mind and the mind of the politician there lies the deepest of all gulfs; and that there is no region of human thought which is so disorderly, so confused, so lawless, so little under the rule of the great principles, as the region of political thought. It must be so, because that disorder and confusion are the inevitable consequence and penalty of the strife for power. You cannot serve two masters. You cannot devote yourself to the winning of power, and remain faithful to the great principles. The great principles, and the tactics of the political campaign, can never be made one, never be reconciled. In that region of mental and moral disorder, which we call political life, men must shape their thoughts and actions according to the circumstances of the hour, and in obedience to the tyrant necessity of defeating their rivals. When you strive for power, you may form a temporary, fleeting alliance with the great principles, if they happen to serve your purpose of the moment, but the hour soon comes, as the great conflict enters a new phase, when they will not only cease to be serviceable to you, but are likely to prove highly inconvenient and embarrassing. If you really mean to have and to hold power, you must sit lightly in your saddle, and make and remake your principles with the needs of each new day; for you are as much under the necessity of pleasing and attracting, as those who gain their livelihood in the street. We all know that the course which our politicians of both parties will take, even in the near future, the wisest man cannot foresee. We all know that it will probably be a zig-zag course; that it will have 'sharp curves', that it may be in self-evident contradiction to its own past; that although there are many honourable and high-minded men in both parties, the interest of the party, as a party, ever tends to be the supreme influence, overriding the scruples of the truer-judging, the wiser and more careful. Why must it be so, as things are to-day? Because this conflict for power over each other is altogether different in its nature to all other—more or less useful and stimulating—conflicts in which we engage in daily life. As soon as we place unlimited power in the hands of those who govern, the conflict which decides who is to possess the absolute sovereignty over us involves our deepest interests, involves all our rights over ourselves,

all our relations to each other, all that we most deeply
cherish, all that we have, all that we are in ourselves.
It is a conflict of such supreme fateful importance, as
we shall presently see in more detail, that once engaged
in it we *must* win, whatever the cost; and we can
hardly suffer anything, however great or good in itself,
to stand between us and victory. In that conflict
affecting all the supreme issues of life, neither you nor
I, if we are on different sides, can afford to be beaten.
Think carefully what this conflict and what the possession of unlimited power in plainest matter of fact
means. If I win, I can deal with you and yours as
I please; you are my creature, my subject for experiment, my plastic material, to which I shall give any
shape that I please; if you win, you in the same way
can deal with me and mine, just as you please; I am
your political plaything, 'your chattel, your anything.'
Ought we to wonder that, with so vast a stake flung
down on the table, even good men forget and disregard
all the restraints of their higher nature, and in the
excitement of the great game become utterly unscrupulous? There are grim stories of men who have
staked body and soul in the madness of their play; are
we after all so much unlike them—we gamesters of
the political table—staking all rights, all liberties, and
the very ownership of ourselves? And what results,
what must result from our consenting to enter into this
reckless soul-destroying conflict for power over each
other? Will there not necessarily be the ever-present,
the haunting, the maddening dread of how I shall deal
with you if I win; and how you will deal with me if
you win? That dread of each other, vague and undefined, yet very real, is perhaps the worst of all the
counsellors that men can admit to their hearts. A man

who fears, no longer guides and controls himself; right and wrong become shadowy and indifferent to him; the grim phantom drives, and he betakes himself to the path—whatever it is—that seems to offer the best chance of safety. We see the same vague dread acting upon the nations. At times you may have an aggressive and ambitious Government, planning a world-policy for its own aggrandizement, that endangers the peace of all other nations; but in most cases it is the vague dread of what some other rival nation will do with its power that slowly leads up to those disastrous and desolating international conflicts. So it is with our political parties. We live dreading each other, and become the reckless slaves of that dread, losing conscience, losing guidance and definite purpose, in our desperate effort to escape from falling under the subjection of those whose thoughts and beliefs and aims are all opposed to our own. True it is that the leaders of a party may have their own higher desires, their own personal sense of right, but it is a higher desire and sense of right which they must often with a sigh—or without a sigh—put away into their pockets, bowing themselves before the ever present necessity of winning the conflict and saving their own party from defeat. The stake is too great to allow room for scruples, or the more delicate balancings of what is right and wrong in itself. We all know—' Need must, when the devil drives.' 'Skin for a skin, what will a man not do for his skin.'

Now let us look how that winning of the political battle has to be done? Winning means securing for our side the larger crowd; and that can only be done, as we know in our hearts, though we don't always put it into words, by clever baiting of the hook which is to catch the fish.   It is of little use throwing the bare hook into the salmon pool; you must have the colours brightly and artistically blended—the colours that suit the particular pool, the state of the water, the state of the weather.   Unless you are learned in the fisherman's art, it is but few fish you will carry home in your basket. So in the political pool you must skilfully combine all the glittering attractions that you have to offer; you must appeal to all the different special interests, using the well chosen lure for each. It is true that there may be exceptional moments with all nations when the political arts lose much of their importance, when some great matter rises above special interests, and the people also rise above themselves. But that is human nature at its best; and not the human nature as we have to deal with it on most days of the week. It is also true that the best men in every party stoop unwillingly; but, as I have said, they are not their own masters; they are acting under forces which decide for them the course they must follow, and reduce to silence the voice within them. They have gone in for the winning of power, and those who play for that stake must accept the conditions of the game. You can't make resolutions—it is said—with rose-water; and you can't play at politics, and at the same time listen to what your soul has to say in the matter. The soul of a high-minded man is one thing; and the great game of politics is another thing. You are now part of a machine with a purpose of its own—not the purpose of serving the fixed and supreme principles—the great game laughs at all things that stand before and above itself, and brushes them scornfully aside, but the purpose of securing victory; and to that purpose all the more scrupulous men must conform, like the weaker brethren, or—as the noblest men do occasionally—stand aside. As our system works, it is the party interests that rule and compel us to do their bidding. It must be so ; for without unity in the party there is no victory, and without victory no power to be enjoyed. When once we have taken our place in the great game, all choice as regards ourselves is at an end. We must win ; and we must do the things which mean winning, even if those things are not very beautiful in themselves. And what is it that we have to do ? In plain words— and plainness of thought, directness of speech, is the only wholesome course—we must buy the larger half of the nation ; and buying the nation means setting up before all the various groups, of which it is composed, the supreme object, the idol of their own special interests. We must offer something that makes it worth while for each group to give us their support, and that something must be more than our rivals offer. Put your own self-interests in the first place, and see that you get them— is the watchword of all politics—though we don't often express it in those crude and unashamed terms. Political art has, like many another accomplishment, its own refinements for half veiling the real meanings. If we wish to do our work in the finer fashion, in the artist's way, we must use the light and skilful hand ; we must mix in the attractive phrases, appeal to patriotic motives, borrow—a little cautiously—such assistance as we can from the great principles—a slight passing bow that does not too deeply commit us to their acquaintance as regards the future—and throw dexterously over it all— as a clever cook introduces into her dishes her choicest seasoning—a flavour of noble and disinterested purpose. It is a fine art of its own, to buy, and at the same time to gild and beautify the buying ; to get the voter into the net, and at the same time to inspire him with the happy consciousness that, whilst he is getting what he wants, he is through it all the devoted patriot, serving the great interests of his country. And then also you must study and understand human nature; you must play—as the skilled musician plays on his instrument—on all the strings—both the higher and lower—of that nature; you must utilize all ambitions, desires, prejudices, passions and hatreds—lightly touching, as occasion offers, on the higher notes. But in this matter, as in all other matters, underneath the fine words, business remains business; and the business of politics is to get the votes, without which the great prize of power could not by any possibility be won. Votes must be had—the votes of the crowd, both the rich and the poor crowd, whatever may be the price which the market of the day exacts from those who are determined to win.

II

So rolls the ball. We follow the inevitable course that seeking for power forces upon us. Politics, in spite of all better desires and motives, become a matter of traffic and bargaining; and in the rude process of buying, we find ourselves treading not only on the interests, but on the rights of others, and we soon learn to look on it as a quite natural and unavoidable part of the great game. Keener and keener grows the competition, more heart and brain-absorbing grows the great conflict, and the people and the politicians cannot help mutually corrupting each other. This buying up of the groups is so distinctly recognized nowadays, that lately a *Times* correspondent—whose letters we read with much interest—speaking of a newly-formed ministry abroad, wrote, with unconscious cynicism, that it would have to choose between leaning on the extreme right or the extreme left.

What then—you may say—are we to believe; that the whole body of those concerned with politics—in which class we almost all in our degree are included——are selfish and corrupt, utterly disregarding and despising the just claims of each other? I hope things are not quite so bad as that. Human nature is a mixed thing, and many of us contrive to think in the nobler way and the smaller way at the same time. There is at least one excuse that may be pleaded for us all. What happens here—as happens in so many other cases—is that carelessly and without reflection we place ourselves under an untrue, a demoralizing and wrong system, that fatally blinds and misleads us, lowers and blunts the better part of our nature, and almost compels us, by the force that it exerts, to follow crooked paths and do wrong things. I have not time to illustrate this simple truth of the sacrifice of character to system; but let me take one instance of the injury that results, whenever we lose our own self-guidance under a system, that is wrong in itself, and, as a wrong system so often is apt to be, despotic in its nature. I think many of us see the existence of this injury as regards character, when we watch that part of fashionable society which makes of organized pleasure-hunting the first occupation—I might almost say the duty—of life. Here also people construct a system which overpowers their individual sense of what is right and useful and fitting; they submit themselves to the tyrannous rule of follies of different kinds, as if they had no judgement, no discriminating sense of their own, and as a consequence become as a mere race of butterflies, losing the higher sense of things, and wasting their lives. In all such instances, where lies the remedy? I think both Mr. Spencer and Mr. Mill would have made the same answer—you can only mend matters by individualizing the individual. It is of little use preaching against any hurtful system, until you go to the heart of the matter, until you restore the individual to himself, until you awaken in him his own perceptions, his own judgement of things, his own sense of right, until you allow what Mr. Spencer called his own apparatus of motive—and not an apparatus constructed for him by others—to act freely upon him—an apparatus that tends sooner or later to work to the better things; and so detach him from his crowd, which whirls him along helplessly, wherever it goes, as the stream carries its unresisting bubbles along with it. There lies the great secret of the whole matter. We have as individuals to be above every system in which we take our place, not beneath it, not under its feet, and at its mercy; to use it, and not to be used by it; and that can only be when we cease to be bubbles, cease to leave the direction of ourselves to the crowd—whatever crowd it is—social, religious, or political—in which we so often allow our better selves to be submerged.

It was for this individualizing of the individual that both Mr. Spencer and Mr. Mill pleaded so powerfully; only in the free individual, self-restraining, self-guiding, that they saw, I think, the hope of true permanent good. They saw that nobody yet has ever been saved—in the best sense—or ever will be saved by vast systems of machinery; Mr. Mill, perhaps, specially looking from the moral point of view, and Mr. Spencer contrasting the intellectual and material consequences of the two opposed systems—self-guidance, and guidance by others.

And here, perhaps, I ought to add a few words. Whilst we lay the heaviest share of blame upon the political system that takes possession of us, and leaves little room for self-guidance, are we to lay no direct blame upon ourselves, for being content to take our place in the system, that few, I think, in calm moments of reflection, can fully justify to their own hearts? Let us be completely frank in this great matter. Is the system of giving away power over ourselves, or seeking to possess it over others, in itself right or wrong? If it is wrong, don't let us make excuses for acquiescing in it; don't let us sigh and feebly wring our hands, confessing the faults and dangers, but pleading that we see no other way before us. Where there is a bad way, there is also a good way, if men once resolutely set themselves to find it. But you may, perhaps, doubt if the system *is* wrong in itself; if it is not merely perverted and turned from its true purpose by our human weaknesses. You may be inclined to plead—'It is true that politicians must suppress a part of their own opinions; it is true that there is a sort of bargaining that goes on among the groups, that in order to gain their own special end, they have to act with other groups—groups which may differ strongly from themselves on some important points; it is true also that the leaders of a party must take all these groups into their calculations; and as our American friends say—placate the interests; but there is not necessarily anything corrupt in such action on the part of either the groups or the politicians, or their leaders, at least so long as we can fairly credit them all with desiring the common good, at the same time as they pursue their own special interests, and doing the best that the situation allows alike for these two ends; even if these ends may occasionally diverge

B

somewhat from each other. Of course we admit that men may be easily tempted to overstep the just and true line, may be tempted in the rivalry of parties, in the strife for power, in the desire to seize the glittering prize, to forget for a while the common good, to push it back into the second place, to be over-keen about their own interests; no doubt the possession of power has its dangers, and tempts many men to say and do what we cannot defend; but we must trust to the general better and wiser feeling of the whole people, or of the whole party, to hold in check these aberrations of some of the fighters, and to strike the balance fairly between the two influences. We must remember that all action in common demands some sacrifices; has its disabilities, as well as its great advantages. We cannot act together, unless there is a considerable—sometimes a large suppression of our own selves. We must accept that bit of necessary discipline; we must be prepared to keep step with the marching—(or ought you to say the manœuvring)—regiment, if we are to achieve anything by united action, and not to remain as separate sticks, that no bond holds together. All through life the same principle runs. In every club, society, joint-stock undertaking, we submit to guidance; we give up a part of our views and desires to gain the more important object—yet when we do so, nobody accuses us of sacrificing our own guiding sense, or of being corrupt, or of entering into a hurtful and dangerous traffic.

Yes—I should reply—but in all these voluntary associations you retain your own free choice; you can enter into them or leave them, as you think right; and that free choice in all these cases is the saving element. But I ought to ask pardon of our friend, the apologist, for interrupting him. 'Even if our political system '—it is our friend who is again speaking—'has its defects—grave defects if you like—still after all, it is the instrument of progress, and we know of no other to take its place. Surely it is more profitable to try to mend its faults, than to quarrel with the whole thing, for which we can see no substitute.' That I think is a fair representation of the way in which many of us look at political life, a way that perhaps supplies us with some momentary consolation, when our minds are troubled with what we see passing before us ; but how far, if we try to see quite clearly, can we accept such reasoning, as giving any real answer to the graver doubts and hesitations ? Is it not only a bit of agreeable sticking-plaster, laid over the sore place, an opiate-like soothing of troubled consciences, hardly intended seriously to touch the deeper part of the matter ? Let us now try to look frankly beneath the surface, and do our best to see what is the true nature of the system in which we so easily acquiesce.

What does representative government mean ? It means the rule of the majority and the subjection of the minority ; the rule of every three men out of five, and the subjection of every two men. It means that all rights go to the three men, no rights to the two men. The lives and fortunes, the actions, the faculties and property of the two men, in some cases their beliefs and thoughts, so far as these last can be brought within the control of machinery, are all vested in the three men, as long as they can maintain themselves in power. The three men represent the conquering race, and the two men—*vae victis* as of old—the conquered race. As citizens, the two men are de-citizenized ; they have lost all share for the time in the possession of their country,

they have no recognized part in the guidance of its
fortunes; as individuals they are de-individualized, and
hold all their rights—if rights they have—on sufferance.
The ownership of their bodies, and the ownership of
their minds and souls—so far as you can transfer by
machinery the ownership of mind and soul from the
rightful owners to the wrongful owners—no more
belongs to them, but belongs to those who hold the
position of the conquering race. Now that is I believe
a true and uncoloured description of the system, as it is
in its nakedness, as it is in its real self, under which
we are content to live. It is not an exaggerated
description—there is not a touch in the picture with
which you can fairly quarrel. It is true that the real
logic of the system does not yet prevail. It is true that
a certain number of things may for a time modify and
restrain the final triumphs of the majority. In some
parliamentary countries, the majority tends to be more
composite in its character than with us, and therefore
tumbles more easily to pieces. On the other hand, with
us at least—whatever it may be in some other countries
that have Parliaments—minorities may rend the air and
reach the skies, if they can, with their cries and
complaints, and so to a certain extent may raise
difficulties—a method of warfare in which all minorities
grow more or less skilful by practice—in the path of the
majority; with us also there still exists happily a
friendlier, more genial spirit between all parts of the
people than prevails in other countries. Thanks to the
fact that the great serpent of bureaucracy holds us as
yet less closely in its folds—thanks to the still lingering
traditions of self-help and voluntary work; thanks to the
good humour and love of fair play, which is to some
extent nursed by our fellowship in the same games that

all classes love—games that I think have redeemed some part of the politician's mistakes,—the rule of the majority is with us as yet more tempered, less violent and unscrupulous, than it is in some other countries; but give their full weight to all these modifying influences, which *as yet* restrain our system of the conquering and the conquered races from finding its full development—still they do not alter the main, the essential fact, that we are content to live under a system that vests the rights of citizenship, the share in thè common country, the ownership of body, faculties, and property, and to some extent, the ownership of mind and soul, of, say, two-fifths of the nation in the hands of the three-fifths. Such is the system in which we think it right and self-respecting to acquiesce—a system which, in the case of every two men out of five, wipes out at a stroke, so far as the duties of citizenship are concerned, and even to a large extent as regards their personal relations, all the higher part of their nature, their judgement, conscience, will—treating them as degraded criminals, who, for some unrecorded offence have deserved to forfeit all the great natural rights, and to lose their true rank as men. They tell us that nowadays men are not punished for their opinions. They succeed in forgetting, I suppose, the case of every two men out five.

Plead then, if you like, on behalf of such a system all the expediencies of the moment, all the conveniences that belong to power, all the pressing things you desire to do through its machinery, plead objects of patriotism plead objects of philanthropy; yet are you right for the sake of these things—excellent as they may be in themselves—to acquiesce in that which—when stripped bare to its real, its lowest terms, is—the words are not too harsh—the turning of one part of the nation into those who own their slaves, and the other part into the slaves who are owned? You may say, as a friend of mine says—'I feel neither like a slave-owner, nor like a slave'—but his feelings, however admirable in themselves, do not alter the system, in which he consents to take part, of trying to obtain control over his fellow men ; and, if he fails, in acquiescing in their control over himself. He may never wish or mean to exercise unfairly the power in which he believes, should it fall into his hands ; but can he answer for himself in the great conflict ; can he answer for his allies, for the great crowd, in which he will count for such a minute fractional part, for what they will do, or where they will go ?

III .

My friend is quite aware, I think, that power is a rather dangerous thing to handle ; but he will handle it with good sense, in the spirit of moderation and fairness, he will not suffer himself to let go of the great principles ; he will not cross the boundary line that divides the rightful from the wrongful use. Well, moderation, and fairness, and good sense are excellent things, not in this matter alone, but in all matters. And so are the great principles ; that is to say, if you see them in all clearness and are determined to follow them. But the saving power of the great principles depends upon how far we loyally and consistently accept them. They can be of little real help and guidance to us if we play and trifle with them, accepting them to-day, and leaving them on one side to-morrow, making them conform, as occasion arises, to our desires and ambitions, and then lightly finding excuses for deserting them whenever we find them inconvenient. Let us once more be quite frank. When we talk of fairness and moderation and good sense, as constituting our defence against the abuse of unlimited power, are we not living in the region of words—using convenient phrases, as we so often do, to smooth over and justify some course which we desire to take, but about which in our hearts we feel uncomfortable misgivings? Let us by all means cultivate as much fairness and moderation as possible—they will always be useful—but don't let our trust in these good things lead us away from the question that—like the Sphinx's riddle—must be answered under penalties from which there is no escape:—Is unlimited power—whether with or without good sense and fairness—a right or wrong thing in itself? Can we in any way make it square with the great principles? Can we morally justify the putting of the larger part of our mind and body—in some cases almost the whole—under the rule of others; or the subjecting of others in the same way to ourselves? If you answer that it is a right thing—then see plainly what follows. You are putting the force of the most numerous, or perhaps of the most cunning, who often lead the most numerous—which, disguise and polish the external form of it as much as you like, will always remain true to its own essentially brutal and selfish nature—in the first place, making of it our supreme principle; and if unlimited power—remember it is *unlimited* power—power to do whatever the governing majority thinks right—is a right thing, must you not leave it—whatever may be your own personal views—to those who possess it to decide how they will employ it? You can't dictate to others, in the hour of their victory, as to what they will do or not do; and they can't dictate to you, in the hour of your victory. Unlimited power—as the term expresses—can only be defined and limited by itself; if it were subject to any limiting principle, it would cease to be unlimited, and become something of a different nature. And remember always—when once you entered into the struggle for the possession of this unlimited power, that you sanctioned its existence, as a lawful prize, for which we may all rightly contend; and if the prize does not fall to you, it will only remain for you to accept the consequences of your consent to take part in the reckless and dangerous competition. By entering into that conflict, by competing for that prize, you sanctioned the ownership of some men by other men; you sanctioned the taking away from some men—say two-fifths of the nation—all the great rights, and the reducing of them to mere cyphers, who have lost power over themselves. Once you have sanctioned the act of stripping the individual of his own intelligence and will and conscience, and of the self-guidance which depends upon these things, you cannot then turn your back upon yourself, and indignantly point to the mass of unhappy individuals who are now writhing under the stripping process. You should have thought of all this before you consented to put up the ownership of the individual to public auction, before you consented to throw all these rights into the great melting-pot. In your desire to have power in your own hands, you threw away all restraints, all safeguards, all limits as regards the using of it; you wanted to be able to do just as you yourself pleased with it, when once you possessed it; and what good reason have you now to complain, when your rivals —or shall I say your conquerors—in their turn do just what they please with it ? You entered into the game with all its possible penalties; you made your bed, it only remains for you to lie on it.

Let us follow a little further this rightfulness of unlimited power in which you believe. If it is a right thing in itself, who shall give any clear and certain rule to tell us when and where it ceases to be a right thing ? Is any right thing by being pushed a little further, and then a little further, and yet a little further, transformed at some definite point into a wrong thing, unless some new element, that changes its nature, comes into the matter ? The question of degree can hardly change right into wrong in any authoritative way, that men with their many varying opinions will agree to accept. We may, and should for ever dispute over such movable boundary lines—lines that each man according to his own views and feeling would draw for himself. If it is right to use unlimited power to take the one-tenth of a man's property, is it also right to take one-half or the whole ? If it is not right to take the half, where is the magical undiscoverable point at which right is suddenly converted into wrong ? If it is right to restrict a man's faculties— not employed for an act of aggression against his neighbour—in one direction, is it right to restrict them in half a dozen or a dozen different directions ? Who shall say ? It is a matter of opinion, taste, feeling. Perhaps you answer—we will judge each case on its merits; but then once more you are in the illusory region of words, for, apart from any fixed principle, the merits will be always determined by our varying personal inclinations. It is all slope, ever falling away into slope, with no firm level standing place to be found anywhere. Nor do I feel quite sure, if we speak the truth, that any of us are much inclined to accept the rule of moderation and good sense in this matter. You and I, who have entered into this great struggle for unlimited power, have made great efforts and sacrifices to obtain it; now that we have won our prize, why should we not reap the full fruits of victory; why should we be sparing and moderate in our use of it? Is not the labourer worthy of his wage; is not the soldier to receive his prize money? If power was worth winning, it must be worth using. If power is a good thing, why should we hold back our hand; why not do all we can with it, and extract from it its full service and usefulness? Our efforts, our sacrifices of time, money and labour, and perhaps of principle—if that is worth counting—were not made for the possession of mere fragmentary pieces of power, but for power to do exactly as we please with our fellow men. It is rather late in the day, now that we have won the stake, to tell us that we must leave the larger part of it lying on the table; that, having defeated the enemy, we must evacuate his territory, and not even ask for an indemnity to compensate us for our sacrifices. If power, as an instrument, is good in itself, now that we hold it in our hand, why break its point and blunt its edge? And then what about the great principles, which my friend does not propose exactly to follow, but on which at all events he will be good enough to keep a watchful eye? Where are they? What are they? What great principle remains, when you have sanctioned unlimited power? You can't appeal to any of the great rights—as rights; the rights of self-ownership and self-guidance, the rights of the free exercise of faculties, the rights of thought and conscience, the rights of property, they are no longer the recognized and accepted rules of human actions; they are now reduced to mere expediencies, to which each man will assign such moderate value as he chooses. You are now out in the great wilderness, far away from all landmarks. Around the throne of unlimited power stretches the vast solitude of an empty desert. Nothing can be fixed or authoritative in its presence; by the fact of its existence, by the conditions of its nature, it becomes the one supreme thing, acknowledging—except perhaps occasionally in courtly phrases for soothing purposes—nothing above itself, writing its own ethics, interpreting its own necessities, making of its own safety and continuance the highest law, and contemptuously dismissing all other discrowned rivals from its presence.

Now turn from the discussion of the moral basis of unlimited power to the practical working of our power-systems. There is I think one blessed fact that runs through all life—that if a thing is wrong in itself, it won't work. No skill, no ingenuity, no elaborate combinations of machinery, will make it work. No amount of human artifice and contrivance, no alliance with force, no reserves of guns and bayonets, no nation in arms even if almost countless in number, can make it work. So is it with our systems of power. They don't work and they can't work. In no real sense, can you, as the autocrat, govern men; in no real sense, can the people imitate the autocrat and govern each other. The government of men by men is an illusion, an unreality, a mere semblance, that mocks alike the autocrat and the crowd that attempt to imitate him. We think in our amazing insolence that we can deprive our fellow men of their intelligence, their will, their conscience; we think we can take their soul into our own keeping; but there is no machinery yet discovered by which we can do what seems to us so small and easy a matter. We think that the autocrat governs his slaves, but the autocrat himself is only one slave the more amongst the crowd of other slaves. In the first place he himself is governed by his own vast machinery; helpless he stands—one of the pitiable objects in this world of ours—in the midst of the countless wheels which he can set in motion, but which other forces direct; and then even the wheels have souls of their own, though not perhaps very beautiful ones, and ever likely to go a persistent and obstinate way of their own; but what is of deeper consequence is that his government is silently conditioned by the slaves themselves. Sunk in their darkness, helpless, inarticulate, they may be; yet for all that they in their turn are slave-owners as well as slaves, as always happens wherever you build up these great fabrics of power. Whilst the slaves obey, they also, though they utter no word, in their turn command. If the autocrat disregards that silent voice, disregards the unspoken conditions that they impose upon him, then in its own due time comes the great crash, and his power passes from him, a broken and miserable wreck. You may crush and hold in subjection for a time the external part of men, but you cannot govern and possess their soul. Their soul lies out of your reach, and is in its nature as ungovernable as the wind or the wave. You may trick and deceive it for a time; you may make it the instrument of its own slavery by cleverly arranged systems of conscription, and other governing devices; you may cast it into a deep sleep, but sooner or later it wakes, and rebels, and claims its own inheritance in itself. In the same way there is no such thing as what is called the self-government of a nation. How can you get self-government by turning one half of a nation into a second-hand copy of a Tsar? That, as Mill showed long ago, is not self-

government ; but government by others. It is true
that here, as with the autocrat, a majority can for
a season use for its own ends and oppress a minority,
can do with it what in its heart it lusts to do, can make
it the *corpus vile* of its experiments, can make of it
a drawer of water and hewer of wood ; but it is only for
a short day. Here again that uncompromising thing,
the soul, stands in the way, and refuses to be transferred
from the rightful to the wrongful owner. The power of
the majority wanes, and the power of the minority grows,
and the oppressor and the oppressed change places.
But apart from all the deeper reasons that make the
subjection of men by men impossible, was there ever
such a hopeless, I might say absurd, bit of machinery—
only to be compared to a child's attempt to put together
a wooden clock out of the chippings left in the wood
basket—as the thing which we call a representative
system ? Invent all the ingenious plans that you like,
but by no possibility can you represent a nation for
governing purposes. The whole thing is a mere phrase.
Let us see what actually happens. Suppose a nation
with 5,000,000 voters—2,000,000 voting on one side, and
3,000,000 on the other. In such a case we start with
the astounding, the absurd, the grotesque fact that there
is no attempt made to represent the 2,000,000. Even if
you had a system of minority representation, it might
possibly serve in some small measure to soothe the
feelings of the subject race ; it would not alter the hard
fact of their subjection. But at present the 2,000,000
voters find no place of any kind in our calculations ;
they are simply swept off the board, not counted. That
is the first remarkable feature of the representative
system ; and that, as you will admit, is not the happiest
beginning with which to start. If representation con-

stitutes the moral basis of power—then the fact, that out of every five men two should be left unrepresented, requires a good deal of explanation ; two-fifths of the moral basis at all events are wholly wanting. We are fond of talking of our representative system as if it rested on a democratic foundation ; but under which of the three great democratic principles—equality, fraternity, liberty—does the sweeping off the board of two-fifths of the nation, the two men out of every five, find its sanction ?

Let us, however, for the present leave the 2,000,000 voters to their fate. They are, as we have seen, only a subject race; and subject races must be duly reasonable, and not expect too great a share in the privileges of conquering races. Now let us turn to the case of the happy triumphant 3,000,000 voters, who hold in subjection the 2,000,000 voters. Are they themselves represented in any true sense? Let us see what happens to them—the majority, who are good enough for a time to take charge of all of us. Unlimited power means that our lords and masters of the moment may deal, that they will probably try to deal, with every, or almost every field of human activity. If there are—say—ten great State departments, such as trade, foreign affairs, local government, home government, and the rest ; and if we suppose with due moderation that there are ten great questions connected with each of these departments, that may at any moment occupy the attention of our presiding majority, then we have a grand total of a hundred questions, upon which the opinions of the 3,000,000 electors will have to be represented. But alas! for our unfortunate and inconvenient human differences ; how can the victorious 3,000,000 be represented on these hundred questions, when, if they think at all, they will all think more or less differently from each other? To express fully their many differences, they ought to have nearly 3,000,000 representatives; but we will not ask for perfection; so let us divide the number by a hundred and say 30,000 representatives —an arrangement which, if the representatives met and talked for twenty hours every day in the year, would give, let us say, something over eight seconds of talking time for each representative during the course of the year as regards each of the hundred questions. When they had each talked their eight or nine seconds, how much real agreement should you expect to find among our 30,000 representatives on their hundred questions? Place twenty men in a room to discuss one subject; and how many different opinions will you collect at the end, if the twenty men are intelligent, and interested in the subject? Will you not probably find three or four groups of opinions, each group representing a more or less different view? Now bring the 30,000 representatives together, and require them to agree, not on one subject, but on a hundred important and often complicated subjects. Remember they *must* agree— they have no choice—that necessity of agreement overrides everything else, for otherwise they cannot act together; but then comes the question—what is their agreement—forced upon them by the practical necessity of acting together as one man—morally worth? Is is not a mere form, a mere mockery, a mere illusion? They must agree; and they do agree; for the continuance of the party system, the winning of power, the subjecting of their rivals—all this depends on their agreeing; but in what sort of fashion, by what kind of mental legerdemain, is their agreement reached? It can only be reached in one simple way—by a wholesale system of self-effacement. The 30,000 individuals must be content on, say, ninety-five per cent. of the hundred questions, to have no opinions ; or if they have opinions, to swallow ninety-five per cent. of their opinions at a gulp, and to play the convenient, if somewhat inglorious part of cyphers. Yet under our system it is this larger half of the nation, these 3,000,000 voters, who have undertaken the responsibility of thinking and acting for the nation, of deciding these hundred questions both for themselves and for the rest of us ; and the only way of deciding left to them is to efface themselves, and have no opinions—a rather sad anti-climax, I am afraid, to some of our everyday rhetoric on the subject of representative systems. If we look closely we find that these systems only mean—that if we have no personal opinions, we can be represented, so far as it is possible or worth while to represent blank sheets of paper ; if we have personal opinions, we can't be represented. The question then forces itself upon us, is it a bit of honest work, is it profitable, is it worth the trouble, to construct a huge machinery for the purpose of representing cyphers, who have no opinions ; and when we have constructed our illusory, our make-believe machine, to go into the market-place, and therefrom deliver ourselves of speeches about the excellence of our self-governing system ? Is it right and true to set up a moral responsibility on the part of those who profess to govern, that cannot by any possibility be turned into a reality ; to ask half the nation to sit in the seat of universal judgement—there to take their part in what is and must be an only half disguised farce ? Does it not tell us something of the true nature of power, when we find ourselves obliged to descend to tricks of this kind in order to possess and to use it ?

Does it mend matters to say that under our system we choose the best man available, and leave the hundred questions for him to deal with? That is only our old friend, the autocrat, come back once more, with a democratic polish rubbed over his face to disguise and, as far as may be, to beautify his appearance. Our sin consists in the suppression of our own selves and our own opinions; and in one sense we fall lower than the slaves of the autocrat, for they are simply sinned against, but we take an active part in the sin against ourselves.

And now how does this suppression of ourselves come about? There must be some powerful motive acting upon us, to induce us to take our place cheerfully in such a poor sort of comedy. Men don't suppress themselves, except to gain something that they much desire. Let us be frank once more, and confess we are bribed into this self-suppression by our reckless desire for power, and our desire to use the power, when gained, for special interests of our own. The power that we seek to win is a hard taskmaster as regards its conditions, and exacts that humiliating price from us. We take our own bribe for giving up our opinions, and play the part of cyphers, and at the same time bribe those others who are to play their part with us; we ask no questions of our conscience, but go on to the political Exchange, and there with a light heart do the necessary selling and buying.

Now follow a little further this process of self-suppression, this process of making the cyphers. When you have once required of men to efface themselves and all the higher part of themselves, in order that they may act together, then follows that bargaining and juggling with the groups, of which I have already spoken. The disinterested opinions—95 per cent. of them, as we

c

calculated—have vanished, much in the same fashion as the 2,000,000 voters vanished; they are swept off the board, as things for which no place can be found, but which are only very much in the way of the real business in hand; and only a few leading self-interests —three or four perhaps—still remain. Now you may bind unbought men together, in the one and true way, by their opinions; but when they have no opinions you must find a cement of a coarser and more material kind. Having once turned men into cyphers, nothing remains but to treat them as cyphers. The great trick —the winning of power—requires cyphers, and can't be played in any other fashion. Having once turned men into cyphers, you must appeal to them as good loyal party followers; or you must appeal to them as likely to get more from you than from any other buyer in the market: you can't appeal to them—except in the imaginative moments when you are treading the flowery paths of rhetoric—as men, possessed of conscience, and will, and responsibility, for in that case they might once more regain possession of their suppressed consciences and their higher faculties, and begin to think and judge for themselves—a result that would have very inconvenient consequences; for then they would no longer agree to have one opinion on the hundred subjects; they would divide and scatter themselves in all sorts of directions; they would be a source of infinite trouble and vexation to the distracted party-managers; they would no longer be of use as fighting material; and the well-disciplined army would dissolve into an infinite number of separate and divergent fragments. No! as long as party faces party, and the great struggle for power goes on, the rank and file, however intelligent, however well-educated, must be content to think with the party. They can't think for themselves, for if they did they would think differently; and if they thought differently, they could not act together; so they must be content to be just war-material, very like the masses of conscripts which foreign governments occasionally employ to hurl against each other. If they were anything else, it would be a very poor fighting show that our political parties would make on their battle-field. The great struggle for power would die out, would come naturally to its end, when the suppression of self and the making of the cyphers had ceased to be.

It is well to notice here that in some other countries you have not two political parties of the same definite character as with us, but a large number of groups. The fact of the groups very slightly affects the situation. Under every system the vices that go with the seeking for power return in pretty nearly the same form. The groups can't form a majority, and obtain power, unless they amalgamate; which means that each group has its market price, makes the best bargain that it can for itself, and for the sake of that bargain consents to act with, and so to increase the strength and influence of those with whom it may be in strong disagreement. Of course hopeless moral confusion arises from this temporary amalgamation of the odds and evens, and separate, unlike pieces, from this making of a common cause by those who mean different things, and are almost as much opposed to each other as they are to the common enemy, to whom for the moment they are opposed. Under no circumstances can we afford to depart from the great principle that we must never abandon our own personality, that we must only strive for the ends in which we ourselves believe, and never consent to enter into combinations, in which we either are used against our convictions, or use others against their convictions. Whenever we descend to 'log rolling'—your services to pay for my services—we are lost in a sea of intrigue and corruption, and all true guidance disappears. There is no true guidance for any of us, except in our own best and highest selves, in our own personal sense of what is true and right. When that goes, there is little, if anything, worth the saving.

And now, passing by many incidents in the working of the great machine, that is so largely indulgent to our fighting and bargaining propensities, I come to what seems to me the very heart of Mr. Spencer's social and political teaching. It is not often given to a man to sum up in three words a great truth, that is fated sooner or later to revolutionize the thought and action of all nations; and yet that is, I think, what Mr. Spencer happily achieved. The three words were—'progress is difference'—that is, if you or I are to think more clearly, or to act more efficiently and more rightly than those who have preceded us, it can only be because at some point we leave the path which they followed, and enter a new path of our own—in other words, we must have the temper and courage to differ from accepted standards of thought and perception and action. If we are to improve in any direction, we must not be bound up with each other in inseparable bundles, we must have the power in ourselves to find and to take the new path of our own. Is not every improvement of machinery and method, every gain made in science and art, every choosing of the truer road and turning away from the false road that we have hitherto trodden—does it not all arise from those differences of thought and perception which, so long as freedom exists, even in its present imperfect forms, are from time to time born amongst us? Whenever men become merely copies and echoes of each other, when they act and think according to fixed and sealed pattern, is not all growth arrested, all bettering of the world made difficult, if not impossible? What hope of real progress, when difference has almost ceased to exist; when men think in the same fashion as a regiment marches; and no mind feels the life-giving stimulating impulse which the varying competing thoughts of others brings with it? Do we not see in some parts of the East, when men are bound rigidly together under one system of thought, how difficult, how painful, the next upward step becomes; and when the change comes, how dissolvent and destructive it tends to be? Do we not see the same thing in Churches and States nearer home—the more that minds are uniformly subjected to one system, the more difficult becomes the adaptation of the old to the new, the more violent revolutionary and catastrophic the change when it takes place? Safety only lies in the constant differences which many living minds, looking from their own standpoint, in turn contribute. All unity, that exists by means of social or artificial restraint of differences, is slowly but inevitably moving towards its own destruction—a destruction that must finally involve much pain and confusion and disorder, because change and adaptation have been so long resisted.

Now if we accept this simple but most far-reaching truth—'progress is difference'—as I think we must do—let us frankly and loyally accept it with all the great consequences which follow from it. If progress is the child of difference, then it is for us to let our social and political systems favour difference to the fullest extent possible. At no point must we imprison minds under those fighting systems, which always

restrain thought and favour mechanical discipline—
fighting is one thing and thinking is another; at no
point must we stereotype action, preventing its natural
and healthy divergence; at no point throw difficulties
in the way of effort and experiment; at no point
de-individualize men by making them dull repetitions
of each other, soulless, automatic cyphers, lost, helpless
in their crowd; but everywhere we must allow the
natural rewards and inducements and motives to act
upon free self-guiding men and women, encouraging
them to feel that the work of improvement, the work
of world-bettering, the achieving of progress, lies in
their own hands, as individuals, and that, if they wish
to share in this great common work, they must strive
individually to live at their best. Throughout the
whole nation, we must let every man and woman,
instead of looking to their parties and parliaments and
governments, feel the full strength of the inspiring
inducement to do something in their own individual
capacities and to join with others in doing something—
the smallest or the greatest thing—better than it has
yet been done, and so make their own contribution to
the great fund of general good. Only so can the
far-reaching powers which lie in human nature, but
which, like the talent, are so often wrapped in the
napkin, hidden and unused, find their full scope and
development; only so can our aims and ambitions be
ennobled and purified; only so can the true respect for
the individuality of others soften the strife of opinions,
and the intolerant spirit in which we so often look
upon all that is opposed to and different from ourselves.
As we recognize and respect the individuality both of
ourselves and others; as we realize that the bettering
of the world depends upon our individual actions and

perceptions; that this bettering can only be done by ourselves, acting together in free combination; that it depends upon the efforts of countless individuals, as the rain-drops make the streams, and the streams make the rivers, that it cannot be done for us by proxy, cannot be relegated, in our present indolent fashion, to systems of machinery, or handed over to an army of autocratic officials to do for us; and as we realize that we shall have failed in our part, have lived almost in vain, if in some direction, in some department of thought or action—whatever it may be—we have not individually striven to make the better take the place of the good; life will become for all of us a better and nobler thing, with more definite aims, and greater incentives to useful action. The work that we do will react on ourselves; and we shall react on the work. Each victory gained, each new thing well done will make the men, the fighters for progress; and as the fighters are raised to a higher capacity, the progress made will advance with bolder, swifter strides, invading in turn every highway and by-way of life. But this healthy reaction cannot be as long as we live under the depressing and dispiriting influence of the great machines, that take the work out of our hands, and encourage in us all a sense of personal uselessness. The appeal must be straight and direct to the individuals, to their own self-direction, their own self-sacrifice, to their own efforts in free unregulated combinations, their own willing gifts and services.

It is in vain that you will ask for the progress, that is born in the conflict of competing thoughts and perceptions, from the great official departments, into whose hands you now so complacently resign yourself. They are incapacitated as instruments of progress by the law of their own being. Whenever you act and think wholesale, and in authoritative fashion for others, you become to a certain extent limited and incapacitated in your own nature. That mental penalty for ever dogs the possession of power. You lose sight of the great and vital ends, and allow the small things to change places with the all-important things. You are no more in touch with the living forces that make for progress. Why? Are the reasons far to seek? The body of officials—however good and honourable in themselves—form a caste, that administers the administered, and does not really share in the actual life of the nation; the chiefs, intent upon the huge machine, which they direct from behind their office windows; the large body, dutifully following their traditions, and clinging to their precedents. They are cut off from all the great inspirations, for the great inspirations are only likely to come to those who share in the active throbbing life that is not found in any one part, but in the whole, of a free nation, and that exists, as we have seen, as the sum of countless differing contributions. The best inspirations only readily come to those who live open to all influences, who are not narrowed and limited by that sense of slightly contemptuous superiority, which we all—however excellent we may be—are apt to feel when we are treating others as passive material under our hands. I doubt if you can ever impose your own will by means of force on others, without acquiring in yourself something of this superior scorn. But this scorn is fatal to the great inspirations, for they are only born in us when we are in truest personal sympathy with the upward movement, whatever it may be, when we ourselves are part of it, when we are thinking and feeling freely, and are surrounded by those thinking and feeling like ourselves, for in real free life we are for ever giving and receiving, absorbing and radiating. There and there only do you get the true soil-bed of progress. Nor, if our official classes were willing to be helped by the thought of others, is it possible. Under their authoritative systems they have made the people helpless, apathetic, indifferent; and so have to carry the great burden of thinking for a nation on their own shoulders alone. Few people really think or perceive, who can give no practical effect to their thoughts and perceptions; and so it is that we see administered nations grow first indifferent, and then revolutionary. It is thus, in this vicious circle, that bureaucracy ever works. Our bureaucrats, with their universal systems, paralyse and benumb the best thought and energies of the nation; and then themselves are mentally starved in the dead-alive condition of things that they have created. Then again our official classes are not only, like the autocrat, controlled and disabled by their own machinery, but they fall—who could help it?—under the drowsy influence of the ever revolving wheels. The habit of doing the one thing in the same fixed way depresses the brighter faculties, and the *vis inertiae* becomes the paramount force. The machinery, on which everything depends, takes the first place; its moral and spiritual effect upon the people take the second or third place, or no place at all. Thus it is that every huge administrative system tends to that barren uniformity which is a kind of intellectual death, and from which that essential element of progress—experiment, is necessarily absent. When you have constructed a universal system, embracing the whole nation, you can't experiment. The thousands of wheels must all follow each other in the same track with undeviating uniformity. Even if your official feelings would allow of such an unorthodox proceeding, it is mechanically very difficult to interfere with the regularity and precision that make the working of universal systems possible. And so it happens that not only is a man with new ideas a real terror inside the walls of a great department, but that there are two phases that succeed each other in turn in the life of these departments. There is the period of somnolence, the mechanical repetition of what had been said and done in past years, the same sending out of the old time-honoured forms, the same pigeon-holing of the answers, the same holding of inspections, the same administering of the nation by the junior clerks; and with it all, complete insensibility as to what influence the system as a whole is exercising on the soul of the people. The daily thought and care of a good official begins and ends with taking precautions that the system, as a system, is working smoothly and without friction. As to what the system is in itself, it is not his province to think, and he very rarely does think. He did not create it; he is not directly responsible for it—as a rule nobody knows who is responsible for it—his work is simply to make the countless wheels duly follow each other with regularity and precision. That somnolent period, however, only lasts for a time; presently comes the revolutionary period of remorse-lessly pulling down and then building up in haste— a period in which the department suddenly awakes from its sleep—aroused perhaps by some external impulse, perhaps by the truer perceptions, or perhaps by the wayward fancies of some Minister, fresh to office, who longs to inaugurate his own little revolution. Then the sleepers become changed into reformers;

and suddenly we are authoritatively assured that we have been following altogether wrong methods, that the old system, under which serious evils have been growing up, must be at once transformed into something of a new and very different order. The nation, dully and dimly aware that things are not as they should be, smiles approvingly, and through its press, faintly applauds; and the plant, perhaps of some twenty years' growth, is straightway torn up by the roots—a fate which after a few years will be again shared by the new thing that now takes its place. It is not the fault of the officials. If you or I were in their place we should be just as somnolent, and just as revolutionary. The fault lies in the great system itself; and few of us could resist the spell that it exercises. The truth is that you can no more administer a whole nation than you can represent it. You cannot deal with human nature wholesale; you cannot throw it higgledy piggledy into one common lot, and let half a dozen men, no better or worse than ourselves, take charge of it. No universal system is a living thing: they all tend to become mere machines—machines of a rather perverse kind, that have incurable tricks of going their own way. We are apt to think that our machines dutifully serve and obey us; but in large measure we serve and obey them. They too have souls of their own, and command as well as obey. Unfortunately for us, progress and improvement are not amongst the things that great machines are able to supply at demand. Their soul lies in mechanical repetition, not in difference; whilst progress requires not only faculties in the highest state of vital activity, but I might almost say continual, mental dissatisfaction with what has been already achieved, and continual preparedness to invade new territory and attempt new victories. Progress depends upon a great number of small changes and adaptations and experiments, constantly taking place—each carried out by those who have strong beliefs and clear perceptions of their own in the matter; for the only true experimenter is he who finds and follows his own way, and is free to try his experiment from day to day. But this true experimentation is impossible under universal systems. An experiment can only be tried on a small scale by those who are the clearer-sighted amongst us, and are aiming at some particular end, and when those who are affected by it are willing to take the risk. You can't rightly experiment with a whole nation; and the consequence is that the sin and mistakes of every universal system go on silently accumulating, until the time comes for the next periodical tearing up by the roots of what exists comes due, and once more we start afresh.

And now there are still many other points on which I must not touch to-day. There is that great subject of excessive public expenditure in all countries, which is like a tide which flows and flows and hardly ever ebbs. A few years ago when some of us began to preach voluntary taxation, as the only effectual means of recovering the gradually disappearing independence of the individual, and of placing governments in their true position of agents, and not, as they are to-day, of autocrats and masters of the nation, and as the plainest and most direct means of making the recognition of the principle of individual liberty supreme in our national life, I found most of my friends quite content to be used as tax-material, even though the sums of money taken from them were employed against their own beliefs and interests. They had lived so long under the system of using others, and then in their turn being used by them, that they were like hypnotized subjects, and looked on this subjecting and using of each other as a part of the necessary and even Providential order of things. The great machine had taken possession of their souls; and they only yawned and looked bored, or slightly scornful at any idea of rebelling against it. In vain we drew the picture of the nobler, happier, safer life of the nation, when men of all conditions voluntarily combined to undertake the great services, class co-operating with class, each bound to the other by new ties of friendship and kindliness, with all its different groups learning to discover their own special wants, to follow their own methods, and make their own experiments. In that way only, as we urged, could we replace the present dangerous and mischief-making strife with blessed fruitful peace, create a happier, better, nobler spirit amongst us all, destroy the old traffic and bargaining of the political market, destroy the fatal belief that one class might rightly prey upon another class, and that all property finally belonged to those who could collect the greater number of votes at the polls. That belief in the omnipotent vote, as we urged, was striking its roots deeper every year—it was the certain, the inevitable result of our party fighting for the possession of power. So long as the vote carried with it the unlimited undefined power of the majority, the giving away of property must always remain as the easiest means of purchasing the owners of the vote; and that belief in the final ownership of property being vested in the voter we could only fight, not by resisting here or there, not by denouncing this or that bit of excessive and wasteful expenditure, but by challenging the rightfulness and good sense of the whole system, by pointing to a truer, nobler, social life, and by resolutely standing on the plain broad principle of individual control over ourselves and our own property.   It was in friendly voluntary co-operation, as free men and women, for all public wants and services ; in taking each other's hands, in sharing our efforts ; it was by destroying the belief in power, the belief in 'pooling' property and faculties, the belief in the false right of some men to hold other men in subjection, and to use them as their material ; in building up the belief in the true rights, the rights of self-owner-ship and self-guidance, apart from which everything tends to the confusion and corruption of public life—it was only so that we could ward off the coming danger and the inevitable strife.   These great national services, that we had so lightly flung into the hands of our officials, were the true means of creating that higher and better national life, with its friendly inter-depen-dence, its need of each other, its respect for each other, which was worth over and over again all the political gifts and compulsions—though you piled them up in a heap as high as Pelion thrown on the top of Ossa.   It was only so that the nation would find its true peace and happiness, and that the smouldering dread and hatred of each other could die out.   The years have passed ; and I think a change of mood has silently come over many persons.   I find that some of those who once clung to compulsion as the saving social bond, as the natural expression of national life, are willing to-day to consider whether some better and truer and safer principle may not be found; are willing to consider, as a practical question, if some limit should not be placed on the power to take and to spend in unmeasured quantity the money of others. Our friend the Socialist has done, and is doing for us his excellent and instructive work. He stands as a very striking— I might say eloquent landmark, showing us plainly enough where our present path leads, and what is the logical completion of our compulsory interferences, our restrictions of faculties, and our transfer of property by the easy—shall I say by the laughable and grotesque —process of the vote? Into our present system, which so many men accept without thinking of its real meaning, and its further consequences, he introduces an order, a consistency, a completeness of his own. His logic is irresistible. If you can vote away half the yearly value of property under the form of a rate, as we do in some towns at present, then under the same convenient and elastic right you can vote away the nine-tenths or the whole. '*Only* logic' perhaps you lightly answer—but remember, unless you change the direction of the forces, logic always tends to come out victorious in the end. Let us then take the bolder, the truer, the more manful course. If we believe in property, as a right and just thing, if, as the product of faculties, we believe it to be inseparably connected with the free use of faculties, and therefore inseparably connected with freedom itself; if we believe that it is a mere bit of word-mockery to tell us—as our Socialist friends do— that they are presenting the world with the newest, the most perfect, the most up-to-date form of liberty, whilst from their heights of scorn for liberty they calmly deny to every man and woman the right to employ their faculties in their own way and for their own advantages, offering us in return a system beyond all words petty and irritating, a system that would provoke rebellion even in the nursery, and which, as a clever French writer wittily remarked, would periodically convulse the State—with the ever-recurring insoluble question—might or might not a wife mend the trousers of her husband; if we believe that the Socialist, treading in the footsteps of his predecessor, the autocrat, has only discovered one more impossible system of slavery, then let us individually do our best to end the great delusion —that has given birth to the Socialist, and made him the power that he is to-day in Europe—that property belongs, not to the property-owner, but to those who are good enough to take the trouble to vote. Don't let us play any longer with these dangerous forces, which, if they win, will for a time wholly change the course of human civilisation; and above all don't let us put it in the power of the voter to turn round some future day and say to us—'As long as it served your interests and ambitions, you acknowledged the supremacy of the vote; you acknowledged this right of taking property from each other. You taught us, you sanctioned, through many years, the principle of unlimited power, vested in some men over other men. Is it not now a little late in the day for you suddenly to cry 'halt' in the path along which you have so long led us, because you see new interests and ambitions taking their place by the side of your own discredited interests and ambitions, which are no longer able to satisfy the heart of the nation? If the old game was good enough and right enough in your hands, when you were our leaders, so is the new game right and good enough in our hands, now that it is our turn to lead.' What true, what sufficient answer would there remain for us to make? Were it not better to repent of our past sins to-day, whilst there is yet time and opportunity to do something to repair them? If we are only to begin to quarrel with power and its consequences when we find that it has already slipped away from our hands, shall we not be too much like the grey-haired sinner who turns saint in that sad period when the pleasures of life have already ceased to exist for him ?   Better to repent whilst there is still something to sacrifice and renounce ; and we can still give some proof that our repentance is the child of real conviction.

Let us try to clear our thoughts, and know our own minds in this great matter.   Do we or do we not mean to consent to that final act in the long drama which is euphemistically called ' the nationalizing of property ' ? If we do not mean to consent to that last crowning act of the process of voting away the property of each other, then it is not only an unworthy weakness on our part, but a cruel wrong to encourage by our words and actions in the mass of the people a belief, which some day, when it grows to its full strength and height, we shall scornfully—whatever our scorn may then avail— disown and reject, forgetting with our changed attitude how we once planted that belief in their hearts, used it, and played with it for the sake of our ambition and our desire to possess power.   When the great bitter strife comes—as it must come—shall we not be constrained with shame to accuse ourselves, and to acknowledge our misleading of the people, our responsibility in the past for the infinite calamities we have brought both upon them and upon ourselves.   Do not let us wait for that future so fraught with evil, which our own careless- ness of thought, our disregard of the great principles, our love of the wildly exciting political game, and our subservience to party interests are preparing for us. The hours of the day are not yet spent.   The temper of our people is a noble generous temper, if you appeal to it in the true way, appealing for right's sake, for principle's sake, not merely for the sake of class or party or personal interests, not merely for the sake of the many pleasant things that belong to the possession of property. Let us make some sacrifice of our political ambitions, and take our stand on the truest, highest ground. Our task is to make it clear to the whole nation that a great principle, that which involves the free use of faculties, the independence of every life, the self-guidance and self-ownership, the very manhood of all of us, that commands and constrains us to preserve the inviolability of property for all its owners—whoever they may be. The inviolability of property is not simply the material interest of one class who happen to-day to possess it, it is the supreme interest of all classes. True material prosperity can only be won by the great body of the nation through the widest measure of liberty—not the half-and-half, not the mock system, that exists at present. Create the largest and most generous system of liberty, create—as you will do with it—the vital energizing spirit of liberty, and in a few short years the working classes would cease to be the propertyless class; would become with their great natural qualities the largest property-owner in the country. But this can only be, as they set themselves in earnest to *make* property instead of *taking* it, and to put the irresistible pence and shillings together for the carrying out of all the great services. This in truth was the splendid campaign on which he had entered, when the politician, sometimes hungering to play the important part, and to exalt his small restless self, some-times misled by nobler dreams, drew his deluding herring across the path, and pointed to the easier down-hill way of the common fund and the all-powerful vote.

It is the politician with his cheap liberality and his giving away of what does not belong to him, who perpetuates the depressed and unprogressive condition of a large part of the people ; he is only too much like those who nurse poverty by their careless and misplaced charity. He stands in the way of the true efforts of the people, of their friendly co-operation, their discovery of all that they could achieve for their own happiness and prosperity, if they acted together in their free self-helping groups. Let us never forget the power of the accumulated pence. If we could persuade a million men and women to lay aside one halfpenny a week, at the end of a year they would have over £100,000 to invest in farms, houses, recreation grounds, in all that they felt they most needed. With the acquisition of property would come many of the helpful and useful qualities—the self-confidence, the faculty of working together, and of managing property, and the proud inspiring ambition to remake in peaceful ways, unstained by any kind of violence, and therefore challenging and encountering no opposing forces, the whole condition of society, as it exists to-day. Such is the goal to which we, who disbelieve in force, must ever point the way. It is for us to show that everything can be gained by voluntary effort and combination, and nothing can be permanently and securely gained by force. In every form, where men hold men in subjection to themselves, force is always organized against itself, is always tending sooner or later to destroy itself. Autocrat, restless politician, or Socialist, they are all only labourers in vain. There is a moral gravitation that in its own time drags all their work remorsely to the ground. Everywhere, across that work, failure is written large. There are many reasons. In the first place, force begets force, and dies by the hand of its own offspring; then those who use force never act long together, for the force-temper leads them to turn their hand against each other; then the continued use of force, as is natural, develops a superhuman stupidity, a failure to see the real meaning and drift of things, in thos who use it; but greatest of all reasons, the soul of man is made for freedom, and only in freedom finds its true life and development. So long as we suppress that true life of the soul, so long as we deny to it the full measure of its freedom, we shall continue to strive and to quarrel and to hate, and to waste our efforts, as we have done through so many countless years, and shall never enter the fruitful path of peace and friendship that waits for us. Once show the people, make it clear to their heart and understanding, that it is liberty alone that can lead us into this blessed path of peace and friendship; that it alone can still the strife and the hatreds; that it alone is the instrument of progress of every kind; that it alone in any true sense can make and hold together and preserve a nation—which, if it rejects liberty, must in the end tear itself to pieces in the great hopeless aimless strife—once show them this supreme truth, feeling it yourself in the very depths of your heart, and so speak to them—and then you will find, as you touch the nobler, more generous part of their nature, that gradually, under the influence of the truer teaching, they will learn to throw aside the false bribes and mischievous attractions of power, and to turn away in disgust from that mad destructive game in which they and we alike have allowed ourselves for a time to be entangled. It is not the Socialist party, it is not any of the Labour parties who have done the most to lead astray the people, and to teach them to believe that political power is the rightful instrument for securing all that their heart desires. These extreme parties have simply trodden more boldly the path in which we went before them. They have only been the pupils—the too apt pupils—in our school, who have bettered our own teaching. It is we, the richer classes, who in our love of power, our desire to win the great game, have done the great wrong, have misled and corrupted the people; and the fault and the blame and the shame will rest in the largest measure with us, when the evil fruit grows from the seed that we so recklessly planted. When the chickens come home to roost, we shall only have to say, as so many have said before us—*tu l'as voulu, Georges Dandin*. Let us then, who have made the great mistake, let us try to redeem it; let us show the people that there is a nobler, happier form of life than to live as two scrambling, quarrelling crowds, mad for their own immediate interests, void of all scruple or restraint. Let us shake ourselves free from this miserable party fighting; let us speak only in the name of the great rights, the great all-guiding, ever-enduring principles; let us oppose the power of some men over other men, as a thing that is in itself morally untrue, untrue from every higher point of view, that is *lèse-majesté* as regards all the best and noblest conceptions of what we are—beings gifted with free responsible souls—as the source of hopeless confusion and scramble and injustice; and let us steadfastly set our faces towards the one great ideal of making a nation, in which all men and women will love their own liberty —without which life is as salt that has lost its savour, and is only fit to be cast away—as deeply as they respect and seek to preserve the liberty of others.

A few words to prevent a possible misunderstanding.

I have not been preaching any form of Anarchy, which
seems to me—even in its most peaceful and reasonable
forms—quite apart from the detestable bomb—merely
one more creed of force (I am not referring here to
such a form of Anarchy—passive resistance under all
circumstances—as Tolstoy preaches, into the consider-
ation of which I cannot enter to-day). Anarchy is a
creed, which, as I believe, we can never rightly class
among the creeds of liberty.   Only in condemning
Anarchy we shall do well to remember that, like Socialism, it is the direct product, the true child of those
systems of government that have taught men to believe
that they may rightly found their relations to each other
on the employment of force.   Both the Anarchist and
the Socialist find some measure of justification in the
practice and teaching of all our modern governments,
for if force is a right thing in itself, then it becomes
merely a secondary question—on which we may all
differ—as to the quantity and quality of it to be employed, the purposes for which we may use it, or in
what hands the employment of it should be placed.
There is, there can be, nothing sacred in the division of
ourselves into majorities and minorities.   You may think
right to take only half a man's property from him by
force; I may prefer to take the whole.   You may think
right to entrust the use of force to every three men out
of five; I may prefer to entrust it—as the Anarchist
does—to each one of the five separately; or as some
Russians and some Germans do, to the autocrat or half-
autocrat, and his all-embracing bureaucracy.   Who
shall decide between us?   There is no moral tribunal
before which you can summon unlimited power, for it
acknowledges, as we have seen, nothing higher than
itself; if it did acknowledge any moral law above itself,

its wings would be clipped, and its nature changed, and it would no longer be unlimited.

Now glance for a moment at the true character of Anarchy, and see why we must refuse to class it among the creeds of liberty, though many of the reasonable Anarchists are inspired, as I believe, by a real love of liberty. Under Anarchy, if there were 5,000,000 men and women in a country, there would be 5,000,000 little governments, each acting in its own case as council, witness, judge, and executioner. That would be simply a carnival, a pandemonium of force; and hardly an improvement even upon our power-loving, force-using governments. Force, as I believe, with Mr. Spencer, must rest, not in the hands of the individual, but in the hands of a government—not to be, as at present, an instrument of subjecting the two men to the three men, not to be exalted into the supreme thing, lifted up above the will and conscience of the individual, judging all things in the light of its own interests, but strictly as the agent, the humble servant of universal liberty, with its simple' duties plainly, definitely, distinctly marked out for it. Our great purpose is to get rid of force, to banish it wholly from our dealings with each other, to give it notice to quit from this changed world of ours; but as long as some men—like Bill Sykes and all his tribe—are willing to make use of it for their own ends, or to make use of fraud, which is only force in disguise, wearing a mask, and evading our consent, just as force with violence openly disregards it—so long we must use *force to restrain force*. That is the one and only one rightful employment of force—force in the defence of the plain simple rights of liberty, of the exercise of faculties, and therefore of the rights of property, public or private, in a word of all the rights of self-ownership

—force used defensively against force used aggressively. The only true use of force is for the destruction, the annihilation of itself, to rid the world of its own mischief-making existence. Even when used defensively, it still remains an evil, only to be tolerated in order to get rid of the greater evil. It is the one thing in the world to be bound down with chains, to be treated as a slave, and only as a slave, that must always act under command of something better and higher than itself. Wherever and whenever we use it, we must surround it with the most stringent limits, looking on it, as we should look on a wild and dangerous beast, to which we deny all will and free movement of its own. It is one of the few things in our world to which liberty must be for ever denied. Within those limits the force, that keeps a clear and open field for every effort and enterprise of human activity—that are in themselves untainted by force and fraud—such force is in our present world a necessary and useful servant, like the fire which burns in the fireplaces of our rooms and the ranges of our kitchen; force, which once it passes beyond that purely defensive office, becomes our worst, our most dangerous enemy, like the fire which escapes from our fireplaces and takes its own wild course. If then we are wise and clear-seeing, we shall keep the fire in the fireplace, and never allow it to pass away from our control.

A PLEA FOR VOLUNTARYISM

WE, who call ourselves Voluntaryists, appeal to you to free yourselves from these many systems of State force, which are rendering impossible the true and the happy life of the nations of to-day. This ceaseless effort to compel each other, in turn for each new object that is clamoured for by this or that set of politicians, this ceaseless effort to bind chains round the hands of each other, is preventing progress of the real kind, is preventing peace and friendship and brotherhood, and is turning the men of the same nation, who ought to labour happily together for common ends, in their own groups, in their own free unfettered fashion, into enemies, who live conspiring against and dreading, often hating each other.

Look at the picture that you may see to-day in every country of Europe. Nations divided into two or three parties, which are again divided into several groups, facing each other like hostile armies, each party intent on humbling and conquering its rivals, on treading them under their feet, as a conquering nation crushes and tramples on the nation it has conquered. What good, what happiness, what permanent progress of the true kind can come out of that unnatural, denational-izing, miserable warfare? Why should you desire to compel others; why should you seek to have power—that evil, bitter, mocking thing, which has been from of old, as it is to-day, the sorrow and curse of the world—

E

over your fellow men and fellow women? Why should you desire to take from any man or woman their own will and intelligence, their free choice, their own self-guidance, their inalienable rights over themselves; why should you desire to make of them mere tools and instruments for your own advantage and interest; why should you desire to compel them to serve and follow your opinions instead of their own; why should you deny in them the soul—that suffers so deeply from all constraint—and treat them as a sheet of blank paper upon which you may write your own will and desires, of whatever kind they may happen to be? Who gave you the right, from where do you pretend to have received it, to degrade other men and women from their own true rank as human beings, taking from them their will, their conscience, and intelligence—in a word, all the best and highest part of their nature—turning them into mere empty worthless shells, mere shadows of the true man and woman, mere counters in the game you are mad enough to play; and just because you are more numerous or stronger than they, to treat them as if they belonged not to themselves, but to you? Can you believe that good will ever come by morally and spiritually degrading your fellow men? What happy and safe and permanent form of society can you hope to build on this pitiful plan of subjecting others, or being yourselves subjected by them?

We show you the better way. We ask you to renounce this old, weary, hopeless way of force, ever tear-stained and blood-stained, which has gone on so long under Emperors and autocrats and governing classes, and still goes on to-day amongst those who, whilst they condemn Emperors and autocrats, continue to walk in their footsteps, and understand and love liberty very little more than those old rulers of an old world. We bid you ask yourselves—'What is all our boasted civilization and gain in knowledge worth to us, if we are still, like those who had not attained to our civilization and knowledge, to hunger for power, still to cling to the ways of strife and bitterness and hatred, still to oppress each other as in the days of the old rulers?' Don't be deceived by mere words and phrases. Don't think that everything was gained when you got rid of autocrat and emperor. Don't think that a change in the mere form—without change in the spirit of men—can really alter anything, or make a new world. A voting majority, that still believes in force, that still believes in crushing and ruling a minority, can be just as tyrannous, as selfish and blind, as any of the old rulers. Happy the nation that escapes from autocrat, from emperor, and from its bureaucratic tyrants; but that is only the beginning of the new good life; that counts only for the first steps in the true path. When that is done, the true goal has still to be won, the great lesson still remains to be learnt. The old curse, the old sorrow, did not simply lie in the heart of autocrat and emperor; it lay in the common desire of men to rule and possess for their own advantage the minds and bodies of each other. It is that fatal, deluding desire which even yet to-day prevents our realizing the true and happy life. As a writer has well said—many nations have been powerful, but has any one of them found the true life—as yet? It is this vainest of all vain desires that we have to renounce, trample upon, cast clean out of our hearts, if we are to win the better things. We have to learn that our systems of force destroy all the great human hopes and possibilities; that as long as we believe in force there can be no abiding peace or friendship between us all; that a half disguised civil war will for ever smoulder in our midst; that each half of the nation must live, as it were, sword in hand, ever watching the other half, and given up, as we said, to suspicion and dread and hatred, knowing that, if once defeated in the great contest, its own deepest beliefs and interests will be roughly set aside and trampled on; that it must accept the hard lot of the conquered, kneeling down in the dust and submitting to whatever its opponents choose to decree for it; that it will have no rights of its own; no rights over its own life, over its own actions and property; no share in the common country, no share in the guidance of its fortunes; no voice in the laws passed; it will be a mere helpless crowd, defranchized, and decitizenized, a degraded and subject race, bound to do the hard bidding of its conquerors. Can you for a single moment believe that the subjecting of others in this conqueror's and conquered fashion is the true end of our existence here, the true fulfilling of man's nature, with all its great gifts and hopes and aspirations?

And are the conquerors in the great conflict better off—if we try to see clearly—than the conquered? We can only answer—No; for power is one of the worst, the most fatal and demoralizing of all gifts you can place in the hands of men. He who has power—power only limited by his own desires—misunderstands both himself and the world in which he lives; he sees through a glass darkly, which dims and perverts his whole vision; he magnifies and exalts his own little self; he fondly imagines he may follow the lusts of his heart wherever they lead him; and disowns the control of the great principles, that stand for ever above us all, and refuses, alike to the autocrat and the voting majority, the rule and the subjecting of the lives of others. If we feel shame and sorrow for those who are subjected, we may feel yet more shame and sorrow for the blind, self-deceiving instruments of their subjection. They in their pride sink to a lower depth than those whom they subject. Better it were to be amongst those who wear the chain than amongst those who bind it on the hands of other men. For those who suffer in subjection there is some hope, some glimmering of light, some teachings that come from the passionate desire for the liberty denied to them ; but for those who cling to and believe in possessing power there is only darkness of soul, where no light enters, until at last, through a long bitter experience, they learn how that for which they sacrificed so much has only turned to their own deepest injury. See how power hardens and brutalizes all of us. It not only makes us selfish, unscrupulous, and intriguing, scornful and intolerant, corrupt in our motives, but it veils our eyes and takes from us the gift of seeing and understanding. Power and stupidity are for ever wedded together. Cunning there may be ; but it is a cunning that in the end tricks and deceives itself. Power for ever tends not only to develop in us the knave, but also to develop the fool. If you wish to know how power spoils character and narrows intelligence, look at the great military empires; their steady perseverance in the roads that lead to ruin ; their dread of free thought and of liberty in all its forms ; look at the sharp repressions, the excessive punishments, the love of secrecy, the attempt to drill a whole nation into obedience, and to use the drilled and subject thing for every passing vanity and aggrandizement of those who govern. Look also at the great administrative systems. See how men become under them helpless and dispirited, incapable of free effort and self-protection, at one moment sunk in apathy, at another moment ready for revolution. Do you wonder that it is so? Is it wonderful that when you replace the will and intelligence and self-guidance of the individual by systems of vast machinery, that men should gradually lose all the better and higher parts of their nature—for of what use to them is that better and higher part, when they may not exercise it? Ought we to feel surprise, when we see them become like over-restrained children, peevish, discontented and quarrelsome, unable to control and direct themselves, and ever loud in their complaints that enough cake and jam do not fall to their share?

Endless are the evils that power brings with it, both to those who rule and are ruled. If you hold power, your first aim and end are necessarily to preserve that power. With power, as you fondly imagine, you possess all that the world has to offer; without power you seem to yourself only portionless, abject, humiliated—the gate flung in your face, that leads to the palace of all the desirable things. When you once play for so vast a stake, what influence can mere right or wrong have in your counsels? The course that lies before you may be right or wrong, tolerant or intolerant, wise or foolish, but the fatal gift of power, that you have been mad enough to desire and to grasp at, gives you no choice. If you mean to have and to hold power, you must do whatever is necessary for the having and holding of it. You may have doubts and hesitations and scruples, but power is the hardest of all taskmasters, and you must either lay these aside, when you once stand on that dangerous, dizzy height, or yield your place to others, and renounce your part in the great conflict. And when power is won, don't suppose that you are a free man, able to choose your path and do as you like. From the moment you possess power, you are but its slave, fast bound by its many tyrant necessities. The slave-owner has no freedom ; he can never be anything but a slave himself, and share in the slavery that he makes for others. It is, I think, plain it must be so. Power once gained, you must anxiously day by day watch over its security, whatever its security costs, to prevent the slippery thing escaping from your hands. You tremble at every shadow that threatens its existence. You are haunted by a thousand dreads and suspicions. It becomes, whether you wish it or not, your first, your highest law, and all other things fall into the second and third place. Once you plunge into this all-absorbing game of striving for power, you must go where the strong tide carries you ; you must put away conscience and sense of right, and play the whole game relentlessly out, with the unflinching determination to win what you are striving for. In that great game there is no room left for inconvenient and embarrassing scruples. You can't afford to let your opponents defeat you and wrest the power that you hold from your hands. You can't afford to let them become your masters and trample, as conquerors, upon all the rights and beliefs that are sacred to you. Whatever the price to pay, whatever sacrifice it demands of what is just and upright and honourable, you must harden your heart, and go on to the bitter end. And thus it is that seeking for power not only means strife and hatred, the splitting of a nation into hostile factions, but for ever breeds trick and intrigue and falsehood, results in the wholesale buying of men, the offering of this or that unworthy bribe, the playing with passions, the poor unworthy trade of the bitter unscrupulous tongue, that heaps every kind of abuse, deserved or not deserved, upon those who are opposed to you, that exaggerates their every fault, mistake, and weakness, that caricatures, perverts their words and actions, and claims in childish and absurd fashion that what is good is only to be found in your half of the nation, and what is evil is only to be found in the other half.

Such are the fruits of the strife for power. Evil they must be, because power is evil in itself. How can the taking away from a man his intelligence, his will, his self-guidance be anything but evil? If it were not evil in itself, there would be no meaning in the higher part of nature, there would be no guidance in the great principles—for power, if we once acknowledge it, must stand above everything else, and cannot admit of any rivals. If the power of some and the subjection of others are right, then men would exist merely as the dust to be trodden under the feet of each other; the autocrats, the emperors, the military empires, the Socialist, perhaps even the Anarchist with his detestable bomb, would each and all be in their own right, and find their own justification; and we should live in a world of perpetual warfare, that some devil, as we might reasonably believe, must have planned for us. To those of us who believe in the soul—and on that great matter we who sign hold different opinions—the freedom of the individual is not simply a question of politics, but it is a religious question of the deepest meaning. The soul to us is by its own nature a free thing, living its life here in order that it may learn to distinguish and choose between the good and the evil, to find its own way—whatever stages of existence may have to be passed through—towards the perfecting of itself. You may not then, either for the sake of advancing your own interests, or for the sake of helping any cause, however great and desirable in itself, in which you believe, place bonds on the souls of other men and women, and take from them any part of their freedom. You may not take away the free life, putting in its place the bound life. Religion that is not based on freedom, that allows any form of servitude of men to men, is to us only an empty and mocking word, for religion means following our own personal sense of right and fulfilling the commands of duty, as we each can most truly read it, not with the hands tied and the eyes blinded, but with the free, unconstrained heart that chooses for itself. And see clearly that you cannot divide men up into separate parts—into social, political and religious beings. It is all one. All parts of our nature are joined in one great unity; and you cannot therefore make men politically subject without injuring their souls. Those who strive to increase the power of men over men, and who thus create the habit of mechanical obedience, turning men into mere State creatures, over whose heads laws of all kinds are passed, are striking at the very roots of religion, which becomes but a lifeless, meaningless thing, sinking gradually into a matter of forms and ceremonies, whenever the soul loses its freedom. Many men recognize this truth, if not in words, yet in their hearts, for all religions of the higher kind tend to become intensely personal, resting upon that free spiritual relation with the great Over-soul—a relation that each must interpret for himself. And remember you can't have two opposed powers of equal authority; you can't serve two masters. Either the religious conscience and sense of right must stand in the first place, and the commands of all governing authorities in the second place; or the State machine must stand first, and the religious and moral conscience of men must follow after in humble subjection, and do what the State orders. If you make the State supreme, why should it pay heed to the rule of conscience, or the individual sense of right ; why should the master listen to the servant ? If it is supreme, let it plainly say so, take its own way, and pay no heed, as so many rulers before them have refused to do, to the conscience of those they rule.

And here we ought to say that amongst those who sign this appeal are some who, like the late Mr. Bradlaugh —a devoted fighter for liberty—reject the doctrine of soul and would not, therefore, base their resistance to State power on any religious ground. But apart from this great difference that may exist between us, we, who sign, are united by the same detestation of State power, and by the same perception of the evils that flow from it. We both see alike that placing unlimited power—as we do now—in the hands of the State means degrading men from their true rank, the narrowing of their intelligence, the encouragement of intolerance and contempt for each other, and therefore the encouragement of sullen, bitter strife, the tricks of the clever tongue, practised on both the poor and rich crowd, and the evil arts of flattery and self-abasement in order to conciliate votes and possess power, the excessive and dangerous power of a very able press, which keeps parties together, and too often thinks for most of us, the repression of all those healthy individual differences that make the life and vigour of a nation, the blind following of blind leaders, the reckless rushing into national follies, like the unnecessary Boer War—that might have been avoided, as many of us believe, with a moderate amount of prudence, patience and good temper—just because the individuals of the nation have lost the habit of thinking and acting for themselves, have lost control over their own actions, and are bound together by party-ties into two great child-like crowds; means also the piling up of intolerable burdens of debt and taxation, the constant and rather mean endeavour to place the heaviest of these burdens on others—whoever the others may be, the carelessness, the high-handedness, the insolence of those who spend money compulsorily taken, the flocking together of the evil vultures of many kinds where the feast is spread, the deep poisonous corruption, such as is written in broad characters over the government of some of the large towns in the United States—a country bound to us by so many ties of friendship and affection, and in which there is so much to admire—a corruption, that in a lesser degree has soiled the reputation of some of the large cities of the Continent, and is already to be found here and there sporadically existing amongst us in our own country; and which only too surely means at the end of it all the setting up of some absolute form of government, to which men fly in their despair, as a refuge from the intolerable evils they have brought upon themselves—a refuge that after a short while is found to be wholly useless and impotent, and is then violently broken up, perhaps amidst storm and bloodshed, to be once more succeeded by the long train of returning evils, from which men had sought to escape in the vain hope that more power would heal the evils that power had brought upon them.

Such are the fruits of power and the strife for power. It must be so. Set men up to rule their fellow men, to treat them as mere soulless material with which they may deal as they please, and the consequence is that you sweep away every moral landmark and turn this world into a place of selfish striving, hopeless confusion, trickery and violence, a mere scrambling-ground for the strongest or the most cunning or the most numerous. Once more we repeat—don't be deluded by the careless everyday talk about majorities. The vote of a majority is a far lesser evil than the edict of an autocrat, for you can appeal to a majority to repent of its sins and to undo its mistakes, but numbers—though they were as the grains of sand on the seashore—cannot take away the rights of a single individual, cannot turn man or woman into stuff for the politician to play with, or over-rule the great principles which mark out our relations to each other. These principles are rooted in the very nature of our being, and have nothing to do with minorities and majorities. Arithmetic is a very excellent thing in its place, but it can neither give nor take away rights. Because you can collect three men on one side, and only two on the other side, that can offer no reason—no shadow of a reason—why the three men should dispose of the lives and property of the two men, should settle for them what they are to do, and what they are to be: that mere rule of numbers can never justify the turning of the two men into slaves, and the three men into slave-owners. There is one and only one principle, on which you can build a true, rightful, enduring and progressive civilization, which can give peace and friendliness and contentment to all differing groups and sects into which we are divided—and that principle is that every man and woman should be held by us all sacredly and religiously to be the one true owner of his or her faculties, of his or her body and mind, and of all property, inherited or—honestly acquired. There is no other possible foundation—seek it wherever you will—on which you can build, if you honestly mean to make this world a place of peace and friendship, where progress of every kind, like a full river fed by its many streams, may flow on its happy fertilizing course, with ever broadening and deepening volume. Deny that principle, and we become at once like travellers who leave the one sure and beaten path and wander hopelessly in a trackless desert. Deny that self-ownership, that self-guidance of the individual, and however fine our professed motives may be, we must sooner or later, in a world without rights, become like the animals, that prey on each other. Deny human rights, and however little you may wish to do so, you will find yourself abjectly kneeling at the feet of that old-world god Force—that grimmest and ugliest of gods that men have ever carved for themselves out of the lusts of their hearts; you will find yourselves hating and dreading all other men who differ from you; you will find yourselves obliged by the law of the conflict into which you have plunged, to use every means in your power to crush them before they are able to crush you; you will find yourselves day by day growing more unscrupulous and intolerant, more and more compelled by the fear of those opposed to you, to commit harsh and violent actions, of which you would once have said 'Is thy servant a dog that he should do these things?'; you will find yourselves clinging to and welcoming Force, as the one and only form of protection left to you, when you have once destroyed the rule of the great principles. When once you have plunged into the strife for power, it is the fear of those who are seeking for power over you that so easily persuades to all the great crimes. Who shall count up the evil brood that is born from power—the pitiful fear, the madness, the despair, the overpowering craving for revenge, the treachery, the unmeasured cruelty? It is liberty alone, broad as the sky above our heads, and planted deep and strong as the great mountains, that allows the better and higher part of our nature to rule in us, and subdues those passions that we share with the animals.

We ask you then to limit and restrain power, as you would restrain a wild and dangerous beast. Make everything subservient to liberty; use State force only for one purpose—to prevent and restrain the use of force amongst ourselves, and that which may be described as the twin-brother of force, wearing a mask over its features, the fraud, which by cunning sets aside the consent of the individual, as force sets it aside openly and violently. Restrain by simple and efficient machinery the force and fraud that some men are always ready to employ against other men, for whether it is the State that employs force against a part of the citizens, or one citizen who employs force or fraud against another citizen, in both cases it is equally an aggression upon the rights, upon the self-ownership of the individual; it is equally in both cases the act of the stronger who in virtue of his strength preys upon the weaker. Safeguard therefore the lives and the property of every citizen against the force or the cunning of Bill Sykes and all his tribe. Make of our world a fair open field where we may all act, according to our own choice, individually, or in co-operation, for every unaggressive purpose, and where good of every kind will fight its own open unrestrained fight with evil of every kind. Don't believe in suppressing by force any form of evil—always excepting the direct attacks upon person and property. An evil suppressed by force is only driven out of sight under the surface—there to fester in safety and to take new and more dangerous forms. Remember that

striking story of the German liberals, when Bismarck
had directed his foolish and useless weapon of repressive
laws against the Socialists. 'You have driven the
Socialists into silence'—they said—'you have forbidden
their meetings and confiscated their papers; yet for all
that the movement goes on more actively than ever
underground and hidden from sight. And we who are
opposed to Socialism are also silenced. We have now
no enemy to attack. The enemy has vanished out of
our sight and out of our reach. How can we answer or
reason with those who speak and write no word in
public, and only teach and make new recruits in secret
and in the dark?'

So it is always. You strike blindly, like a child in its
passion, with your weapons of force, at some vice, at
some social habit, at some teaching you consider dangerous, and you disarm your own friends who would fight
your battle for you—were they allowed to do so—in the
one true way of discussion and persuasion and example.
You prevent discussion, and the expression of all
healthier opinion, you disarm the reformers and paralyse
their energies—the reformers who, if left to themselves,
would strive to move the minds of men, and to win their
hearts, but who now resign themselves to sleep and to
indifference, fondly believing that you with your force
have fought and won their battle for them, and that
nothing now remains for them to do. But in truth you
have done nothing; you have helped the enemy. You
may have made the outside of things more respectable
to the careless eye, you may have taught men to believe
in the things that seem, and in reality are not; but you
have left the poisonous sore underneath to work its own
evil undisturbed, in its own way and measure. The evil,
whatever it was, was the result of perverted intelligence

or perverted nature; and your systems of force have left that intelligence and that nature unchanged; and you have done that most dangerous of all things—you have strengthened the general belief in the rightfulness and usefulness of employing force. Do you not see that of all weapons that men can take into their hands force is the vainest, the weakest? In the long dark history of the world, what real, what permanent good has ever come from the force which men have never hesitated to use against each other? By force the great empires have been built up, only in due time to be broken into pieces, and to leave mere ruins of stones to tell their story. By force the rulers have compelled nations to accept a religion—only in the end to provoke that revolt of men's minds which always in in its own time sweeps away the work of the sword, of the hangman and the torture-table. What persecution has in the end altered the course of human belief? What army, used for ambitious and aggressive purposes, has not at last become as a broken tool? What claim of a Church to exercise authority and to own the souls of men has not destroyed its own influence and brought certain decay on itself? Is it not the same to-day, as it has been in all the centuries of the past? Has not the real prosperity, the happiness, the peace of a nation increased just in proportion as it has broken all the bonds and disabilities that impeded its life, just in proportion as it has let liberty replace force; just in proportion as it has chosen and established for itself all rights of opinion, of meeting, of discussion, rights of free trade, rights of the free use of faculties, rights of self-ownership as against the wrongs of subjection? And do you think that these new bonds and restrictions in which the nations of to-day have allowed themselves to be entangled—the conscription which sends men out to fight, consenting or not consenting, which treats them as any other war-material, as the guns and the rifles dispatched in batches to do their work ; or the great systems of taxation, which make of the individual mere tax-material, as conscription makes of him mere war-material ; or the great systems of compulsory education, under which the State on its own unavowed interest tries to exert more and more of its own influence and authority over the minds of the children, tries—as we see specially in other countries—to mould and to shape those young minds for its own ends—'Something of religion will be useful—school-made patriotism will be useful—drilling will be useful'—so preparing from the start docile and obedient State-material, ready made for taxation, ready made for conscription—ready made for the ambitious aims and ends of the rulers—do you think that any of these modern systems, though they are more veiled, more subtle, less frank and brutal than the systems of the older governments, though the poison in them is more thickly smeared with the coating of sugar, will bear different fruit, will work less evil amongst us all, will endure longer than those other broken and discredited attempts, which men again and again in their madness and presumption have made to possess themselves of and to rule the bodies and minds of others ? No! one and all they belong to the same evil family ; they are all part of the same conspiracy against the true greatness of human nature ; they are all marked broad across the forehead with the same old curse ; and they will all end in the same shameful and sorrowful ending. Over us all is the great unchanging law, ever the same, unchanged and unchanging, regardless of all our follies and delusions, that come and go, that we are not to take possession of and rule the body and mind of others ; that we are not to take away from our fellow-beings their own intelligence, their own choice, their own conscience and free will ; that we are not to allow any ruler, be it autocrat, emperor, parliament, or voting crowd, to take from any human being his own true rank, making of him the degraded State-material that others use for their own purposes.

'But'—some of your friends may say—'look well at the advantages of this State-force. See how many good things come to you by taking money out of the pockets of others. Would the rich man continue to serve your needs, if you had not got your hands upon him, and held him powerless under your taxation system ? No ! He would be only too glad to find an escape from it. Keep then your close grips upon him, now that you once hold him in it ; and by more and more skilful and searching measures relieve him of what you want so much, and what is merely super-fluous to him. Why spare your beast of burden ? What is the use of your numbers, of your organiza-tions, of the all-powerful vote, that can alone equalize conditions, making the poor man rich, and the rich man poor, if you are tempted to lay the useful weapon of force aside ? Force in the old days was used against you ; it is your turn now to use force, and spare not. Think well of what the vote can do for you. There lies the true magician's wand. You want pensions, provision for old age and sickness, land, houses, a minimum wage, lots and lots of education, breakfast and dinner for the children who go to school, scholar-ships for the clever pupils, libraries, museums, public halls, national operas, amusements and recreations of all kinds, and many another good thing which you will easily enough discover when you once begin to help yourselves—for, as the French say, the appetite comes with the eating; and there stand the richer classes with their laden pockets, only encumbered with the wealth that, if they knew it, they would be better without, defenceless, comparatively few and weak, with no power to stand against the resistless vote, if you once turn your strength to good account and learn how to organize your numbers for the great victory. Of course they will give you excellent reasons why you should keep your hands off them, and let them go free. Don't be fooled any longer by mere words. Force rules everything in this world; and to-day it is at last your turn to use force, and enter into possession of all that the world has to offer.'

We answer—that all such language is the language of passionate unthinking children, who, regardless of right or wrong, with no questions of conscience, no perception of consequences, snatch at the first glittering thing that they see before them; that those who once listen to these counsels of violence would be changed in their nature from the reasonable man to the unreasonable beast; that all such counsels mean revolt against the great principles, against the honest and true methods that alone can redeem this world of ours, that, if faithfully followed, will in the end make a society happy, prosperous and progressive in its every part, ever levelling up, ever peacefully redistributing wealth, ever turning the waste places of life into the fruitful garden. But in violence and force there is no redemption. Force—whether disguised or not under the forms of voting—has but one meaning. It means universal confusion and strife, it means flinging the sword—that has never yet helped any of us—into the scale and preparing the way for the utterly wasted and useless shedding of much blood. Even if these good things, and many more of the same kind, lay within your grasp, waiting for your hand to close upon them, you have no right to take them by force, no right to make war upon any part of your fellow citizens, and to treat them as mere material to serve your interests. The rich man may no more be the beast of burden of the poor man, than the poor may be the beast of burden of the rich. Force rests on no moral foundations; you cannot justify it; it rests on no moral basis; you cannot reconcile it with reason and conscience and the higher nature of men. It lies apart in its own evil sphere, separated by the deepest gulf from all that makes for the real good of life—a mere devil's instrument. Even if force to-morrow could lay at your feet all the material gifts which you rightly desire, you may not, you dare not, for the sake of the greater good, for the sake of the higher nature that is in all of us, for the sake of the great purposes and the nobler meanings of life, accept what it offers. Our work is to make this life of ours prosperous, happy and beautiful for all who share in it, working with the instruments of liberty, of peace, and of friendship—these and these only are the instruments which we may rightly take in our hands, these are the only instruments that can do our work for us.

Those who bid you use force are merely using language of the same kind as every blood-stained ruler has used in the past, the language of those who paid their troops by pillage, the language of the war-loving German general, who in old days looked down from the heights surrounding Paris, and whispered with a gentle sigh—'What a city to sack!' It is the language

of those who through all the past history of the world
have believed in the right of conquering, in the right
of making slaves, who have set up force as their god,
who have tried to do by the violent hand whatever
smiled to their own desires, and who only brought
curses upon themselves, and a deluge of blood and
tears upon the world. Force—whatever forms it takes
—can do nothing for you. It can redeem nothing; it
can give you nothing that is worth the having, nothing
that will endure; it cannot even give you material
prosperity. There is no salvation for you or for any
living man to be won by the force that narrows rights,
and always leaves men lower and more brutal in
character than it found them. It is, and ever has been
the evil genius of our race. It calls out the reckless,
violent, cruel part of our nature, it wastes precious
human effort in setting men to strive one against the
other; it turns us into mere fighting animals; and
ends, when men at last become sick of the useless
strife and universal confusion, in 'the man on the black
horse' who calls himself and is greeted as 'the saviour
of society'. Make the truer, the nobler choice. Resist
the blind and sordid appeal to your interests of the
moment, and take your place once and for good on the
side of the true liberty, that calls out all the better and
higher part of our nature, and knows no difference
between rulers and ruled, majorities and minorities,
rich and poor. Declare once and for good that all men
and women are the only true owners of their faculties, of
their mind and body, of the property that belongs to
them; that you will only build the new society on the
one true foundation of self-ownership, self-rule, and
self-guidance; that you turn away from and renounce
utterly all this mischievous, foolish and corrupt business

of compelling each other, of placing burdens upon each
other, of making force, and the hateful trickery that
always goes with it, into our guiding principles, of
treating first one set of men and then another set of
men as beasts of burden, whose lot in life it is to serve
the purposes of others.   True it is that there are many
and many things good in themselves which you do not yet
possess, and which you rightly desire, things which the
believers in force are generous enough to offer you in
any profusion at the expense of others; but they are
merely cheating you with vain hopes, dangling before
your eyes the mocking shows of things that can never
be. Force never yet made a nation prosperous. It
has destroyed nation after nation, but never yet built
up an enduring prosperity. It is through your own
free efforts, not through the gifts of those who have
no right to give them, that all these good things can
come to you; for great is the essential difference
between the gift—whether rightly or wrongly given—
and the thing won by free effort. That which you
have won has made you stronger in yourselves, has
taught you to know your own power and resources, has
prepared you to win more and more victories. The
gift flung to you has left you dependent upon others,
distrustful and dispirited in yourselves. Why turn to
your governments as if you were helpless in yourselves? What power lies in a government, that does
not lie also in you? They are only men like you—men,
in many ways disadvantaged, overweighted by the
excessive burdens they have taken on themselves,
seldom able to give concentrated attention to any one
subject, however important; necessarily much under
the influence of subordinates, from whom they must
gather the information on which they have to act;

often turned from their own course by the dissensions
and differences of their followers; always obliged to
plan and manœuvre in order to keep their party
together, and then losing their own guiding purpose,
and tempted into misleading and unworthy courses;
often deciding the weightiest matters in a hurry, as in
the case of the famous 'Ten Minutes Reform Bill';
and physically leading a life which over-taxes health
and endurance with the call made upon it, by the cares
of their own office, their attendance far into the night
at the House, their social occupations, the necessity to
follow carefully all that is passing in the great theatre
of European politics, and of studying the questions
which each week brings with it.   Think carefully, and
you will feel that all these rash attempts of the handful
of men, that we call a government, to nurse a nation
are a mere delusion.   You can't throw the cares and
the wants and the hopes of a whole people on some
sixteen or eighteen over-burdened workers.   You might
as well try to put the sea into a quart pot.   A handful
of men can't either think or act for you.   Their task
is impossible.   If they try to do so, they can only be
as blind guides who lead blind followers into the ditch.
It all ends in scramble and confusion, in something
being done in order to have something to show, in
great expectations and woeful disappointments, in rash
action and grievous mistakes, resulting from hurry and
over-pressure and insufficient knowledge, which lead
the nation in wrong directions, and bring their long
train of evil consequences.   Why place your fortunes,
all that you have, and all that you are, in other hands?
You have in yourselves the great qualities—though still
undeveloped—for supplying in your own free groups
the growing wants of your lives.   You are the children

of the men who did so much for themselves, the men who broke the absolute power; who planted the colonies of our race in distant lands, who created our manufactures, and carried our trade to every part of the world; who established your co-operative and benefit societies, your Trade Unions, who built and supported your Nonconformist Churches. In you is the same stuff, the same power to do, as there was in them; and if only you let their spirit breathe again in you, and tread in their footsteps, you may add to their triumphs and successes tenfold and a hundredfold. As the French well say:—'Ou les pères ont passé, passeront bientôt les enfants' (Where the fathers passed, there soon shall the children pass). To this point—the work to be undertaken in your own free groups, without any compulsion and subjection of others, we will return later.

But nothing can be well and rightly done, nothing can bear the true fruit, until you become deeply and devotedly in love with personal liberty, consecrating in your hearts the great and sacred principle of self-ownership and self-direction. That great principle must be our guiding star through the whole of this life's pilgrimage. Away from its guiding we shall only continue to wander, as of old, hopelessly in the wilderness. For its sake we must be ready to make any and every sacrifice. It is worth them all—many times worth them all. For its sake you must steadily refuse all the glittering gifts and bribes which many politicians of both parties eagerly press upon you, if you will but accept them as your leaders, and lend them the power which your numbers can give. Enter into none of these corrupt and fatal compacts. All such leaders are but playing with you, fooling you for their own ends. In the pride and vanity of their hearts they wish to bind you to them, to make you dependent upon them. You are to fight their battles, and you will be paid in return much in the same manner as the old leaders paid their soldiers by giving them a conquered city to sack. Can any real good come to you by following that unworthy and mercenary path? When once you have become a mere pillaging horde, when once you have lost all guidance and control and purpose of your own, bound to your leaders, and dependent on them for the sake of the spoils that they fling to you, do you think that any of the greater and nobler things of life will still be possible to you? The great things are only possible for those who keep their hearts pure and exalted, and their hands clean, who are true to themselves, who follow and serve the fixed principles that are above us all, and are our only true guides, who never sell themselves into the hands of others. Your very leaders, who have cheated you, and used you, will despise you; and in your own hearts, if you dare honestly to search into them, you will despise yourselves. But your self-contempt will hardly help you. You will have lost the great qualities of your nature; the old corrupt contract, into which you have entered, will still bind you; you may in your wild discontent revolt against your leaders; but as in the legends of the evil controlling spirit, that both serves and enslaves, you will each be a fatal necessity to the other. You have linked your fortunes together, and it will be hard to dissolve the partnership. Remember ever the old words—as true to-day as when they were first spoken—'What shall it profit a man if he gain the whole world, and lose his own soul?' If you lose all respect for the rights of others, and with it your own self-respect, if you lose your own sense of right and fairness, if you lose your belief in liberty, and with it the sense of your own worth and true rank, if you lose your own will and self-guidance and control over your own lives and actions, what can all the buying and trafficking, what can all the gifts of politicians give you in return? Why let the true diamond be taken from you in exchange for the worthless bit of glass? Is not the ruling of your own selves worth a hundred times this mad attempt to rule over others? If your house were filled with silver and gold, would you be happy if your own self no more belonged to you? Have you ever carefully thought out what life would be like under the schemes of the Socialist party, who offer us the final, the logical completion of all systems of force? Try to picture the huge overweighted groaning machine of government; the men who direct it vainly, miserably struggling with their impossible task of managing everything, driven for the sake of their universal system to extinguish all differences of thought and action, allowing no man to possess his own faculties, or to enjoy the fruit that he has won by their exercise, to call land or house or home his own, allowing no man to do a day's work for another, or to sell and buy on his own account, denying to all men the ownership and possession of either body or mind, necessarily intolerant, as the Tsar's government is intolerant, of every form of free thought and free enterprise, trembling at the very shadow of liberty, haunted by the perpetual terror that the old love of self-guidance and free action might some day again awake in the breast of men, obliged to exercise a discipline, like that which exists in the German army, from fear that the first beginning of revolt might prove the destruction of the huge trembling ill-balanced structure, with no sense of right,—right a mere word that would be lost to their language—but only the ever present, ever urgent necessities of maintaining their unstable power, which was always out of equilibrium, always in danger, because opposed to the essential nature of men—that unconquerable nature, which has always broken and will always break in its own time these systems of bondage. Picture also the horde of countless officials, who would form a bureaucratic, all-powerful army, vast as that which exists in Russia, and probably as corrupt—for the same reason—because only able to fulfil their task, if allowed to have supreme unquestioned power; always engaged in spying, restraining, and repressing, for ever monotonously repeating, as if they governed a nursery—'Don't, you mustn't;' and then picture imprisoned under the bureaucratic caste a nation of dispirited cyphers—cyphers, who would be as peevish, discontented and quarrelsome as shut-up children, because shut off by an iron fence from all the stimulating influences of free life, and forbidden, as if it were a crime, to exercise their faculties according to their own interests and inclinations; picture also the intense, the ludicrous pettiness that would run through the whole thing. As a French writer (Leroy Beaulieu) wittily said—it would be a great State question, ever recurring to trouble the safety of the trembling quavering system, whether or no a wife should be allowed to mend the trousers of her husband. Who could exorcise and lay to rest that insoluble problem, for if the wife were once allowed to perform this bit of useful household duty, might not the whole wicked unsocialistic trade of working for others, in return for their sixpences and shillings, come flowing back with irresistible force? Such is the small game that you are obliged to hunt, such are the minute pitiful necessities to which you are obliged to stoop, when once you construct these great State machineries, and take upon yourself, in your amazing and ignorant presumption, to interfere with the natural activities of human existence.

See also another truth. There are few greater injuries that can be inflicted on you than taking out of your hands the great services that supply your wants. Why? Because the healing virtue that belongs to all these great services—education, religion, the winning of land and houses, the securing greater comfort and refinement and amusement in your lives—lies in the winning of these things for yourselves by your own exertions, through your own skill, your own courage, your friendly co-operation one with another, your integrity in your common dealings, your unconquerable self-reliance and confidence in your own powers of doing. This winning, these efforts, are the great lessons in life-long education; that lasts from childhood to the grave; and when learnt, they are learnt not for yourselves alone, but for your children, and your children's children. They are the steps and the only steps up to the higher levels. You can't be carried to those higher levels on the shoulders of others. The politician is like those who boasted to have the keys of earth and heaven in their pocket. Vainest of vain pretences! The keys both of heaven and earth lie in your own pocket; it is only you—you, the free individuals—who can unlock the great door. All these great wants and services are the means by which we acquire the great qualities which spell victory; they are the means by which we become raised and changed in ourselves, and by which, as we are changed, we change and remake all the circumstances of our lives. Each victory so gained prepares the way for the next victory, and makes that next victory the easier, for we not only have the sense of success in our hearts, but we have begun to acquire the qualities on which it depends. On the other hand the more of his ready-made institutions the politician thrusts upon you, the weaker, the more incapable you become, just because the great qualities are not called out and exercised. Why should they be called out? There is no need for them; their practice-ground is taken away; and they simply lie idle, rusting, and at last ceasing to be. Tie up your right hand for three months and what happens? The muscles will have wasted, and your hand will have lost its cunning and its force. So it is with all mental and moral qualities. Given time enough, and a politician with his restless scheming brain and his clumsy hands would enfeeble and spoil a nation of the best and truest workers. He is powerless to help you; he can only stand in your way, and prevent your doing.

Refuse then to put your faith in mere machinery, in party organizations, in Acts of Parliament, in great unwieldy systems, which treat good and bad, the careful and the careless, the striving and the indifferent, on the same plan, and which on account of their vast and cumbrous size, their complexity, their official central management, pass entirely out of your control. Refuse to be spoon-fed, drugged and dosed, by the politicians. They are not leading you towards the promised land, but further and further away from it. If the world could be saved by the men of words and the machine-makers, it would have been saved long ago. Nothing is easier than to make machinery; you may have any quantity of it on order in a few months. Nothing is easier than to appoint any number of officials. Unluckily the true fight is of another and much sterner kind; and the victory comes of our own climbing of the hills, not by sitting in the plain, with folded hands, watching those others who profess to do our business for us. Do you think it likely or reasonable, do you think it fits in with and agrees with your daily experience of this fighting, working world of ours, that you could take your chair in the politician's shop, and order across his counter so much prosperity and progress and happiness, just as you might order cotton goods by the piece or wheat by the quarter? Be brave and clear-sighted, and face the stern but wholesome truth, that it is only you, you with your own hands, you with your unconquerable resolve, without any dependence on others, without any of these childish and mischievous party struggles, which are perhaps a little more exciting than cricket, or football, or even 'bridge' to some of us, but a good deal more profitless to the nation than digging holes in the earth and then filling them up again, without any use of force, without any oppression of each other, without any of these blind reckless attempts to humiliate and defeat those who hold different beliefs from our-selves, and who desire to follow different methods from those which we follow, without any division of the nation into two, three or more hostile camps, ever inspired with dread and hatred of each other—it is only you yourselves, fighting with the good, pure, honest weapons of persuasion and example, of sympathy and friendly co-operation—it is only you, calling out in yourselves the great qualities, and flinging away all the meaner things, the strifes, the hates, the jealousies, the mere love of fighting and conquering—it is only you, treading in the blessed path of peace and freedom, who can bring about the true regeneration of society, and with it the true happiness of your own lives.

And through it all avoid that favourite, that much loved snare of the politician, by which he ever seeks to rivet his hold upon you, refuse to attack and weaken in any manner the full rights of property. You, who are workers, could not inflict on your own selves a more fatal injury. Property is the great and good inducement that will call out your efforts and energies for the remaking of the present form of society. Deprive property of its full value and attractiveness, and we shall all become stuff only fit to make the helpless incapable crowd that the Socialist so deeply admires, and hopes so easily to control. But it is not only for the sake of the 'magic of property', its power to call out the qualities of industry and saving; it is above all because you cannot weaken the rights of property without diminishing, without injuring that first and greatest of all possessions—human liberty; it is for that supreme reason that we must resist every attempt of the politician to buy votes by generously giving away the property that does not belong to him. The control of his own property by the individual, and the liberty of the individual can never be separated from each other. They must stand, or fall, together. Property, when earned, is the product of faculties, and results from their free exercise; and, when inherited, represents the full right of a man, free from all imaginary and usurped control of others, to deal as he likes with his own. Destroy the rights of property, and you will also destroy both the material and the moral foundations of liberty. To all men and women, rich or poor, belong their own faculties, and as a consequence, equally belongs to them all that they can honestly gain in free and open competition, through the exercise of those faculties.

It is idle to talk of freedom, and, whilst the word is on one's lips, to attack property. He who attacks property, joins the camp of those who wish to keep some men in subjection to the will of others. You cannot break down any of the defences of liberty, you cannot weaken liberty at any one point, without weakening it at all points. Liberty means refusing to allow some men to use the State to compel other men to serve their interests or their opinions; and at what-ever point we allow this servitude to exist, we weaken or destroy in men's minds the sacredness of the principle, which must be, as regards all actions, all relations, our universal bond. But it is not only for the sake of liberty—though that is far the greater and higher reason—it is also for the sake of your own material progress—that you, the workers, must resolutely reject all interference with, all mutilations of the rights of property.

For the moment the larger part of existing property belongs to the richer classes; but it will not be so, as soon as ever you, the workers, take out of the hands of the politicians, and into your own hands, the task of carving out your own fortunes. The working body of the people must no longer be content—not for a single day—to be the property-less class. In every city and town and village they must form their associa-tions for the gaining of property; they must put their irresistible pence and shillings together, so that, step by step, effort upon effort, they may become the owners of land, of farms, of houses, of shops, of mills, and trading ships; they must take shares in the great well-managed trading companies and railways, until the time comes, as their capital increases, when they will be able to become the owners at first of small trading concerns, established by themselves, and then later of larger and more important concerns. They must— for all reasons, the best and the second best—become the owners of property. Without property no class can take its true place in the nation. They must devote much of their resolution and self-denial to the steady persistent heaping together of the pence and shillings for this purpose. As they become possessed of property, they will see a definite goal lying before themselves—one good and useful ambition ever succeeding to another. The old dreary hopelessness will disappear, they will gain in power and influence; the difference between classes will disappear; they will break the enfeebling and corrupting influence of the politicians —what influence would remain to the man of words if he could no longer offer gratis—in return for nothing but votes—the property of others, without any greater exertion on the part of the people than marking their voting papers in his favour? And with the acquiring of property, the workers will also acquire the qualities that the management of property brings with it; whilst they add a new interest, a new meaning to their lives. We appeal to the many thousands of strong, capable, self-denying men that are to be found among us. Is the gaining of property only a dream; is the thing so very difficult, so far out of your reach? Say that a million men and women begin to-morrow to subscribe one halfpenny a week—who would miss that magical halfpenny, which is to transform so many things?—at the end of the year you will have a fund of over £100,000 to start with—not we think, a bad beginning for the great campaign. In many cases the property, such as land and houses, that you would so acquire, you would probably rent or redistribute on remunerative but easy terms to your own members; in the case of workers in towns, you would be able to allow those of your members who desired rest and change, to work for a time on your farms, and you would also be able to make a holiday ground and common meeting-place of some farm that belonged to you, and that could be easily reached by that true instrument of social progress for men and women, the bicycle. Many will be the new forms of health and comfort and amusement that will become possible to you, when once you steadily determine to pile the pence and the shillings together for becoming owners of property; and when once you have put your hand to this good work, you must not relax your efforts until you have become, as you will become before many years have passed, the greatest of property holders in the nation. All is possible to you if you resolutely fling away from you the incitements to strife, the tamperings with liberty and individual property, and pile up the pence and the shillings for the acquiring of your own property. Resist, therefore, all reckless, unthinking appeals made to you to deprive the great prize of any part of its attractions. If you surround property with State restrictions, interfere with free trade and any part of the open market, interfere with free contract, make compulsory arrangements for tenant and landowner, allow the present burdens of rate and tax to discourage ownership and penalize improvements, you will weaken the motives for acquiring property, and blunt the edge of the most powerful material instrument that exists for your own advancement. Only remember—as we have said—that great as is your material interest in safeguarding the rights of individual property, yet higher and greater are and ever will be the moral reasons that forbid our sanctioning any attack upon it, or our suffering State burdens and restrictions and impediments to grow round it. True liberty—as we said—cannot exist apart from the full rights of property; for property is—so to speak—only the crystallized form of free faculties. They take the name of liberty in vain,— they do not understand its nature, who would allow the State—or what goes by the name of the State—the worthy eighteen or twenty men who govern us—to play with property. Everything that is surrounded with State restrictions, everything that is State-mutilated, everything taxed and burdened, loses its best value, and can no longer call out our energies and efforts in their full force. Preserve, then, at its best and strongest the magic of property; leave to it all its stimulating and transforming virtues. It is one of the great master keys that open the door to all that in a material sense you rightly and proudly wish to do and to be.

Many other points remain; we can only touch here on a few of them. Keep clear of both political parties, until one of them seriously, earnestly, with deep conviction, pledges itself to the cause of personal liberty. At present they are both of them opportunist, seeking power, rejecting fixed principles. It is true that we owe great debts to the Liberal party in the past, but at present it is deserting its own best traditions, ceasing to guide and inspire the people, fighting the downhill not the uphill battles, and intent on playing the great game. Some day, as we may hope, it may refind its better self and breathe again the spirit of true exalted leadership, and regardless of its own fortunes for the hours place itself openly on the side of Mr. Spencer's 'widest possible Liberty'. But to-day both parties mean anything or nothing; they represent only too often mere scrambling, mere lust for power. It is true that one or other of the two parties may mean to you some of the things that you yourselves mean, but it will also mean a great many things that you do not mean. They both believe in subjecting some men to the will of other men, in using the State as the instrument of universal force, and you cannot rightly take your place in their ranks, or fight with them. Have nothing to do with the scramble for power. Hold on your own course and stand 'foursquare to all the winds'. Pick out your boldest and most resolute men, and fight every by-election. Don't fight to win, but fight to teach and inspire. The more resolutely you stand on your own ground, the more men of both parties, who begin to see the worthlessness and the mischief of these party conflicts, and the growing danger of using force, will come to you and join your small army. Few as you are to-day, you are stronger than the huge ill-assorted crowds—representing many conflicting opinions—that stand opposed to you, for no one can measure the strength that a great and true cause, devotedly followed, gives to those who consistently serve it. Fight the battle of liberty at every point. Give your best help to those who are resisting municipal trading, or resisting interference with home work, or resisting the placing of power in the hands of the medical or any other profession. You must not confer any form of authority or monopoly on any profession; you must not give to any of them the power to force their services upon us. Let every profession that will, organize itself and make rules for its own members; but we, the public, must remain free in every respect to take or to leave what they offer to us. The monopolies that they all so dearly love are fatal to their own efficiency, and to their own higher qualities, as well as full of danger to the public. We all lose our best perceptions, we all become intellectually hide-bound, we all begin to believe that the public exist for us, exist for our professional purposes, whenever we are protected by a monopoly. In the same way never hand over any question to be decided by those who are called experts. The knowledge of the experts is very useful and valuable, but wisdom and discernment and well balanced judgement are different things from knowledge, and they do not always keep company. Knowledge is great, some one has written, but prejudice is greater. The experts are excellent as advisers, but never as authoritative judges, allowed to stand between the public and the questions that affect its interest. The real service that the experts can perform for us is to place their knowledge in the clearest and simplest form before us all, and to explain their reasons for advising a certain course. There is no limit to the mistakes that the most learned men may make when they are allowed to deliver judgement behind closed doors, when they are not called upon to submit their reasons to open discussion, and to justify publicly the counsels that they offer.

Strive also to make this great Empire of ours an instrument of help and usefulness and friendliness for the whole world. It is a great world-trust placed in our hands, that we must interpret in no selfish and narrow, in no boastful and vainglorious spirit. Cast away all the tawdry and sordid dreams of an Empire stronger than all other nations; but let it rest on the one true foundation of peace and friendship, and as far

as lies with you of free intercourse between all nations—
an Empire of equal generous rights, with no privileges
reserved for any of us. So, and only so, shall this
great Empire endure, saved from the fate that has so
justly swept away all the other great Empires, that were
founded on meaner and more selfish conceptions.
Have nothing to do with this pitiful cowardly un-
English war against the aliens. Even if your interests
should seem to suffer for awhile—which there is strong
reason for believing would not be the case—we ask you
to make this sacrifice for the sake of the liberty of
all, even the poorest, and for the sake of the proud
traditions of our race. Unswerving, disinterested
devotion to the principle of universal liberty, and to
those noble traditions that have always opened the
gates of this country to the suffering and oppressed,
will far, far outbalance any hurt that may for a time
result from the presence with us of the suffering and
oppressed. Plead always that there should be no
unworthy exceptions; all such exceptions are bad in
themselves, and have the bad habit of becoming the
rule. The temper of timorous selfishness that would
exclude any aliens, that would treat any natives as
different from our own flesh and blood, is our real
danger—the danger that threatens our true greatness.
Indulge that temper in any one direction, and you will
presently encourage it to become the evil genius of the
nation.

Lastly, let us all work together, to soften and improve
the relations of capital and labour. War between
capital and labour is only too like the unreasonable and
disastrous war between nations, or between parties in
a nation. All war is a crime, and, as all crimes are,
a mischievous folly—in almost all cases a mere outburst

of childishness. Everywhere we have to learn the wise art of pulling in friendly forbearing fashion with each other, and not against each other; everywhere we have to learn to abandon the useless wasteful brutal methods of war, and to enter the blessed and fruitful paths of peace. Is there any war of any kind, that might not have been avoided by better temper, more patience, and a stronger love of peace? Is there any war, excepting on very rare occasions the wars to repel invasion or the attacking of great human rights, that in the end has not brought disappointment and sorrow, and bitter fruits of its own, as much or even more to the nation that was successful, as to the nation that was unsuccessful? And who profits from these great labour contests, and the stirring of hurtful passions, that goes with them? Friendship, friendly co-operation, the making of common cause for common ends, are the true ends to be aimed at between labour and capital; and each contest makes the good day of reconciliation more difficult, puts it further and further from us. We cannot choose in this great matter. There is only one way. We *must* be friends. Nothing less than honest heartfelt friendship will mend the old evils, and make the happier future. As we asked, who profits by these contests? If you— the workers—win to-day, the capitalists organize themselves to-morrow more strongly than before; if the capitalists win, the workers in the same way strengthen their fighting forces. And so—just as between nations —runs for ever the vicious circle. And as with the nations, so our labour strife is not only lost and wasted, but it fatally injures both sides alike—both the conquerors and the conquered. Let us then love and honour peace, cling to her, open our hearts to her, make sacrifices for her, bear and forbear for her sake, place her great ends before everything else, and resolve that, as far as lies with us, her happy reign shall at last be established over the whole land. Peace—always hand-in-hand with her great twin-sister liberty—not only represents the higher meaning of our moral life, but also like liberty represents the greatest material interest that the workers have ; their industry and skill will never bear their full fruits as long as we cling to war, and the destructive methods of force. Capital and labour, like the rest of us, must obey the great moral law and tread in the path of peace and friendship. It is their duty, as it is the duty of all of us in the other relations of life— worthy of every effort, of all patience and sacrifice on our part. Only with peace can the true prosperity come. With peace and friendship, trade and enterprise would develop a much more vigorous life, and find for themselves many new directions. Nothing limits enterprise so fatally, and with it the employment of the workers, as the dissensions and quarrels between capital and labour. With peace and friendship not only does more and more capital flow into trade and production ; but new enterprises are confidently undertaken in every direction ; and then, as the consequence, wages rise in the one true healthy manner—with the security that peace brings, capital bidding against capital, and the capitalist accepting lower profits. All insecurity, all disturbance of trade relations, must be paid for, and they are paid for by the worker ; for insecurity and uncertainty mean that a higher rate of profit is necessary to tempt the investment of capital lying idle, and there- fore necessarily results in lower wages.

Reorganize then your trade societies on a peace basis, or establish new unions on that basis. Preserve your independence ; but do all in your power to enter

into friendly alliances with capital. Remember that
friendship is the triumph of good sense and wise
temper; strife is the indulgence of the undisciplined,
the childish part of our nature. Form associations in
which both the workers and the capitalists would be
represented; where they would meet and take common
action, as friends, working together to make the
conditions of labour better, more comfortable, more
sanitary, and using every peace expedient to remove
difficulties as they arise. If times of depression come,
and wages fall low, use the common fund to draft away
some of the workers, find temporary employment for
them on the farms and lands that you will acquire as
your own, start workshops of your own, which in some
cases might provide articles of home use and comfort for
your members; and let your unemployed members in
turn receive a grant to enable them to spend their
unoccupied time usefully in study and education. At
present an unoccupied workman wastes time and temper
during a slack time. Like his own tools he rusts and
deteriorates with them. Why should that be so?
Have your own classes and day schools, and let the
unoccupied men turn the time to golden use. But
through it all, even if you strike, refuse as a matter
of principle, as faithful followers of liberty in everything,
to use any of the old bad methods of force. If, after
every effort, after attempting mediation and arbitration,
you cannot agree about wages with the employers, and if
you think it wise and right and necessary to do so, throw
up your work; but if there are those who will take the
wage that you are unwilling to take—let them do so, without let or hindrance. It is their right; and we must never
deny or fight against a human right for the sake of what
seems to be our interest of the moment. We say what

H

' seems ' to be ; for in the end you will gain far more by
clinging faithfully to the methods of peace and respect
for the rights of others than by allowing yourselves
to use the force that always calls out force in reply,
always brings its own far-reaching hurtful consequences,
for the sake of the advantage or victory of the moment.
Once be tempted to use force, and force will become your
master, your tyrant, tempting you again and again to seek
its aid and to enter its service.   No man employs force
to-day without being easily persuaded to use it once more
to-morrow, and then again the next day.   There are in
all that we do only two ways—the way of peace and
co-operation, the way of force and strife.   Can you
hesitate between them ?   Do not good sense and right
sense plead for the one and against the other ?   Set
yourselves then to discover and practise every concili-
atory method ; wherever practicable, become share-
owners and partners in the concerns where you labour,
and make it your pride to join hands frankly with the
employers, wiping out for ever the old disastrous war
feeling, that has brought so much useless suffering and
loss with it.

Remember, also, as another great and vital interest, to
keep a free and open market in everything.   Only so
again can you get the fullest return of your labour.
High wages are of little profit, when prices rule high,
and production becomes a dull monopoly, benumbing
the best energies of the producers.   Under a monopoly
we all grow stupid, unperceiving, apathetic, given up to
routine.   Leave all traders free to bring to your door
the best articles that the world produces at the lowest
cost.   If they are better and cheaper than what you
produce, they will be the truest incentive for greater
exertions both on your part and on the capitalist's part.

It is only the coward's policy to kneel down in the dust, and wail, and confess inferiority, as regards the producers of other nations. Take up the challenge bravely, from whatever quarter it comes; improve method and process and machinery—above all improve the relations between capital and labour; on that, more perhaps than on anything else, industrial victory depends. Be willing to learn from all, of any country, who have anything useful to teach. Never be tempted to build Chinese walls for your protection, and to go indolently to sleep behind them. Your system of free trade is another great world-trust placed in your hands. You stand before all nations holding a bright and shining light, that if you are true to the great destiny of our country you will never allow to be dimmed or extinguished. Mr. Cobden spoke the truth when he said that you would convert the other nations to your own brave way of competition; only he did not allow enough for all the reactionary influences, the narrow unenlightened so-called patriotism, the timidities of some traders and their desire to take their ease comfortably, and not to over-exert themselves, so long as they could compel the public to buy at their own price, and to accept their own standard of good workmanship, the warlike Emperors, the Chauvinists of all countries, the extravagant spendings with the resulting difficulties of getting blood from a stone, and the temptation of scraping revenue together in any mischievous fashion that offered itself, the party intrigues, the effort to discover something that would serve as an attractive policy, the unavowed purpose of some politicians, living for party, and keen for power, to bind a large part of the people by the worst of bonds to their side by means of a huge and corrupt money interest. But the consequences of protection are fighting their battle everywhere on the side of free trade—as the consequences of folly and blindness always fight on the side of the better things; and if we remain faithful to our great trust will in their due time fulfil Mr. Cobden's words. The high prices and dear living, the harassing interferences with trade, the rings and corners, the trickeries and corruption, that all tread so close on the heels of protection, the wild extravagance, the domineering insolent attitude of the State-made monopolists, the ever-growing power of the governments to go their own way, where they can gather vast sums of money so easily through their unseen tax collectors, the ever spreading Socialism, that is only protection made universal—all these things are preaching their eloquent lesson, and slowly preparing the way in other countries for free trade. Sooner or later the world after years of bitter experience learns to unmask all the impostor systems that have traded on its hopes and passions and fears. The thin coating wears off, and the baser metal betrays itself underneath. So it will fare with the Protection, that asks you to be credulous enough to tie up your left hand in order that your right hand may work more profitably. It is true that in protected countries the wages of the workers may be pushed up higher than in the case of free trade countries, but life will remain harder and more difficult. Why? Because, as we have said, prices rule so high; corners and combinations flourish; trickery and corruption find their opportunity; more vultures of every kind flock to the feast; and with the feast of the vultures the burden of rates and taxes becomes intolerable. The whole thing hangs together. Establish freedom and open competition in everything, and all forms of trade and enterprise, all relations of men to each other, tend to become healthy and vigorous, pure and clean. The better and more efficient forms—as they do throughout nature's world—slowly displacing the inefficient forms. It must be so ; for in the fair open fight the good always tend to win over the bad, if only you restrain all interferences of force. It is so with freedom every-where and in all things. Freedom begets the conflict ; the conflict begets the good and helpful qualities ; and the good and helpful qualities win their own victory. They must do so ; for they are in themselves stronger, more energetic, more efficient, than the forces—the trickeries, the corruptions, the timidities, the selfishness —to which they are opposed. The same truth rules our good and bad habits. Only keep the field open and allow the fair fight, and the bad at last must yield to the good. Sooner or later the time comes when the clearer sighted, the more rightly judging few denounce some evil habit that exists ; gradually their influence and example act on others in ever-widening circles, until many men grow ashamed of what they have so long done, and the habit is abandoned. Such is the uni-versal law of progress, which prevails in everything, so long as we allow the free open fight between all good and evil. But in order that the good may prevail there must be life and vigour in the people, and this can only be where freedom exists. If freedom does not exist, if life and vigour have died, then protection—whatever its form—cannot prevent, it can only put off for a short time the inevitable ruin and disaster. Nations only continue to exist as long as they keep in themselves the great simple virtues. As we have seen again and again, they go to pieces, and yield their places to others when once the fatal corruption takes root in their character ; corruption can only be fought by liberty with its strengthening, raising, purifying influences. Protection, that is artificial in its nature, protection that rests on force, always means, if long enough continued, failure and death in the end ; for it prevents our developing the qualities which can alone enable us to keep our place in a world that never stands still. As Mr. Darwin pointed out so clearly those races of plants and animals which for a time were protected by mountains or desert or an arm of the sea, were doomed to fail when at last they came into competition with the unprotected forms. So is it with us men. If you wish to understand the deadly influences of protection, if you wish for a practical example, look carefully at all the distorted and perverted growths of trade enterprise that exist in some protected countries, the unwholesome combinations, the universal selfish scramble, the poisonous mixture of politics and trade influences, the use of the State power to watch over and favour great moneyed monopolies, the long endurance of the public that tolerates the vilest things at the hands of its politicians, and you will realize how deadly is every form of protection, that resting on force sends us to sleep, and how vital is the liberty that for ever fights the evil by opposing it to the good, that never sleeps, that is always stirring us into new forms of doing and resisting, and for ever tends to make the better take the place of the good. There is only one true form of protection, and that is universal liberty with its ceaseless striving and effort.

Strongly as we are opposed to the Protectionists, who whitewash their creed under the name of Tariff Reform, it is fair to remember one plea on their behalf. They have one true grievance. As long as the present extravagant spending goes on in its compulsory fashion they may fairly complain that the income-tax payers are

likely to be unjustly treated.   The remedy does not lie
in extending our compulsory system of taking from the
public but in limiting it, and presently transforming it
into voluntary giving.   Under our compulsory system
free trade will never be a safe possession.   It is with us
to-day; it will be lost to-morrow.   If we were pushed
again into a war, as we were pushed headlong into the
Boer War, just because one statesman got into a temper,
shut his eyes and put his head down, and another statesman looked sorrowfully on, like the gods of Olympus,
smiling at the follies of the human race, we should at
once hear the double cry ringing in our ears for conscription and protection—conscription to force us to fight with
our conscience or against our conscience; protection to
force us to pay for what we might look on as a crime
and a folly.   You may be sure that free trade will
sooner or later be swept away, unless we go boldly
forward in its own spirit and in its own direction and
destroy the compulsory character of taxation.   There
lies the stronghold of all war and strife and oppression
of each other.   As long as compulsory taxation lasts—
in other words giving power to some men to use other
men against their beliefs and their interests—liberty
will be but a mocking phrase.   Between liberty and
compulsory taxation there is no possible reconciliation.
It is a struggle of life and death between the two.
That which is free and that which is bound can never
long keep company.   Sooner or later one of the two
must prevail over the other.   If a war came, conserva-
tive ministers would see their great opportunity, and
with rapture of heart would fasten round us the two
chains that they dearly love, conscription and protection.
Liberal ministers would sorrowfully shake their heads,
wring their hands, utter a last pathetic tribute to liberty

and free trade, and with handkerchiefs to their eyes would take the same course. If you mean to secure the great victory just gained for free trade you must go boldly and resolutely on in the same good path. Dangers lie strewn around you on every side. There is no security for what you have gained, but in pressing forward. There is one and only one way of permanently saving free trade, and that is to sweep away all the compulsory system in which we are entangled.

And now place before yourselves the picture of the nation that not simply out of self-interest but for rights' sake and conscience sake took to its heart the great cause of true liberty, and was determined that all men and women should be left free to guide themselves and take charge of their own lives; that was determined to oppress and persecute and restrain the actions of no single person in order to serve any interest or any opinion or any class advantage; that flung out of its hands the bad instrument of force—using force only for its one clear, simple and rightful purpose of restraining all acts of force and fraud, committed by one citizen against another, of safeguarding the lives, the actions, the property of all, and thus making a fair open field for all honest effort; think, under the influences of liberty and her twin-sister peace—for they are inseparably bound together—neither existing without the other—how our character as a people would grow nobler and at the same time softer and more generous—think how the old useless enmities and jealousies and strivings would die out; how the unscrupulous politician would become a reformed character, hardly recognizing his old self in his new and better self; how men of all classes would learn to co-operate together for every kind of good and useful purpose; how, as the results of this free co-operation, innumerable ties of friendship and kindliness would spring up amongst us all of every class and condition, when we no longer sought to humble and crush each other, but invited all who were willing to work freely with us; how much truer and more real would be the campaign against the besetting vices and weakness of our nature, when we sought to change that nature, not simply to tie men's hands and restrain external action, no longer setting up and establishing in all parts of life that poor weak motive—the fear of punishment—those clumsy useless penalties, evaded and laughed at by the cunning, that have never yet turned sinner into saint; how we should rediscover in ourselves the good vigorous stuff that lies hidden there, the power to plan, to dare and to do; how we should see in clearer light our duty towards other nations, and fulfil more faithfully our great world-trust; how we should cease to be a people divided into three or four quarrelsome unscrupulous factions—ready to sacrifice all the great things to their intense desire for power—and grow into a people really one in heart and mind, because we frankly recognized the right to differ, the right of each one to choose his own path because we respected and cherished the will, the intelligence, the free choice of others, as much as we respect and cherish these things in ourselves, and were resolved never to trample, for the sake of any plea, for any motive, on the higher parts of human nature, resolved that—come storm or sunshine—we would not falter in our allegiance to liberty and her sister peace, that we would do all, dare all and suffer all, if need be, for their sake, then at last the regeneration of society would begin, the real promised land, not the imaginary land of vain and mocking desires, would be in sight.

And now for the practical measures that we must set before ourselves :—

(1) So far as force is concerned, we must use State force only to protect ourselves against those who would employ force or fraud; using it to safeguard all public and private property, and to repel if a real necessity arises the foreign aggressor. We must employ force simply as the servant of liberty, and under the strongest conditions that liberty would impose upon it; we must refuse utterly and in everything to employ it so as to deprive the innocent and unaggressive citizen of his own will and self-guidance.

(2) We must place limits upon every form of compulsory taxation, until we are strong enough to destroy it finally and completely; and to transform it into a system of voluntary giving. Under that voluntary system alone can a nation live in peace and friendship and work together happily and profitably for common ends. In voluntary taxation we shall find the one true form of life-long education which will teach us to act together, creating innumerable kindly ties between us all which will call out all the truest and most generous qualities of our best citizens, doubling and trebling their energies, as they find themselves working for their own beliefs and ideas, and no longer used as the mere tools and creatures of others; which will slowly bring under the influence of the better citizens the selfish and the indifferent, teaching them too to share in public move-ments, and common efforts; which will multiply those differences of method, those experiments made from new points of view—experiments, upon which all pro-gress depends, and replacing the great clumsy universal systems which treat good and bad alike, which are mere developments of the official mind, and escape entirely

from the control of those in whose interest they are supposed to exist; which will call into life again the proud feeling of self-help and independence which belongs to this nation of ours, and which the politician has done so much to weaken and destroy.

The great choice lies before you. No nation stands still. It must move in one direction or the other. Either the State must grow in power, imposing new burdens and compulsions, and the nation sink lower and lower into a helpless quarrelling crowd, or the individual must gain his own rightful freedom, become master of himself, creature of none, confident in himself and in his own qualities, confident in his power to plan and to do, and determined to end this old-world, profit-less and worn-out system of restrictions and compulsions, which is not good or healthy even for the children. Once we realize the waste and the folly of striving against each other, once we feel in our hearts that the worst use to which we can turn human energies is gaining victories over each other, then we shall at last begin in true earnest to turn the wilderness into a garden, and to plant all the best and fairest of the flowers where now only the nettles and the briars grow.

We wish it to be understood that we who sign this paper are in agreement with its general spirit, reserving our own judgement on special points.